4 first place
health

simple ideas for

healthy living

First Place 4 Health
Houston, Texas, U.S.A.
www.FirstPlace4Health.com
Printed in the U.S.A.

Caution: The information contained in this book is intended to be solely for
informational and educational purposes. It is assumed that the First Place 4 Health
participant will consult a medical or health professional before beginning this or any
other weight-loss or physical fitness program.

contents

Foreword by Carole Lewis. 5

Section One: Emotional Well-Being

The Challenge to Change 9

Letting Others Help You Succeed. 14

Overcoming Stress 17

How to H.A.L.T. Defeat. 21

Relapse Prevention 23

Section Two: Spiritual Well-Being

The Faith Factor 28

Making Time for Bible Study and Prayer. 31

Steps for Spiritual Growth 35

Accepting God's Gracious Invitation 38

Restoration and Forgiveness 41

The Lordship of Christ 45

Section Three: Mental Well-Being

You Are Unique. 50

A Healthy Body Image 53

Healthy Living on the Job. 56

Healthy Strategies for Social Situations 61

Keeping the Goal in Mind 65

Your Learning Style 69

Creating a Thankfulness Journal 77

Your Personality Profile 83

Section Four: Physical Well-Being

Nutrition

Dietary Supplements—Miracle or Myth? 104

10 Red Flags of Junk Science 109

The Whole Story on Whole Grains 113

The Facts on Fats 118

Choosing High-Fiber Foods. 127

Outsmarting the Snack Attack 131

Sweetness by Any Other Name 135

The Truth About Fad Diets 141

Understanding Vitamins and Minerals 145

Choosing Better Beverages. 151

An Ounce of Prevention

Controlling Cholesterol 158

Preventing Cancer 163

Preventing Diabetes 168

Preventing Heart Disease 172

Preventing Osteoporosis 177

Understanding High Blood Pressure 183

What's Cooking?

Adding Flavor the Healthy Way 187

Convenience Foods—Making the Most of Your Time 191

Dining on the Go 196

Physical Fitness

The Amazing 10-Minute Workout. 202

Testing Your Health-Related Fitness 205

Monitoring Your Exercise Intensity. 212

Buying Home Equipment 215

Choosing a Personal Trainer 217

Born to Run? 220

Making a Splash 225

Bicycling Your Way to Health and Fitness. 228

Exercising Safely Outdoors 233

Staying Active While Traveling 237

foreword

When First Place 4 Health was introduced in March 1981, most people thought healthy living consisted only of attending to the physical aspect of life. Yet the 12 men and women who wrote the original program knew that the total person must be addressed, even though the wealth of resources we have today were not available at that time. Today, so much more is known about how to live a healthy life spiritually, mentally and emotionally, as well as physically.

Simple Ideas for Healthy Living is a collection of writings about every conceivable area of wellness that teaches the reader how to live a healthy lifestyle in all areas of life. These writings have been collected from authorities in their field of expertise. Medical doctors, exercise professionals, registered dietitians, Christian psychologists and addictions counselors have all contributed some of the best information available today.

If you asked me what I love most about the First Place 4 Health program, I would have to say the balanced life I live today because of the teachings I have learned to incorporate into my lifestyle. These changes did not happen overnight; they have taken years. The beautiful part of a balanced life is that the stresses we all experience do not cause us to derail when these principles of balance are embedded deep down in our heart.

I have experienced firsthand what it means to face serious illness and death—my husband, Johnny, has battled stage-4 prostate cancer since 1997, and our daughter Shari was killed by a drunk driver in November 2001. It would be impossible to maintain balance every day without the help of our Lord Jesus Christ. He has used the tenets of the First Place 4 Health program to teach me what a balanced life looks like, and I live each day with great joy.

If you are involved in a First Place 4 Health group, you will learn about the information shared within the pages of this book as part of the program. If you're not involved in a group, you can read on your own and find a wealth of information to help you learn how to live a balanced, healthy lifestyle.

Carole Lewis
First Place 4 Health Director Emeritus

section one
Emotional Well-Being

the challenge
to change!

C hange is never easy. In fact, most people who are successful in changing a lifestyle habit make several attempts before reaching their goal. The main thing is to keep trying; if you really want to change, you *can* do it. The following statistics reveal how difficult it is to make lasting changes in lifestyle habits:

- More than 50 percent of people who start an exercise program drop out within the first three to six months.[1]

- About 66 percent of people who lose weight through dieting gain it back within one year, and almost all the weight is regained within 5 years.[2]

- Each year, about 34 percent of America's 50 million smokers try to quit smoking. But only about 5 percent of those attempts are successful, says the American Lung Association.[3]

- According to an Opinion Research Corporation survey, only 45 percent of people set New Year's resolutions in 2005. About 8 percent of those surveyed said they achieve the resolutions they set.[4]

The keys to successful lifestyle change are *staying on track* when times get tough and *bouncing back* after a setback. The only way to succeed is to realize that you will be tempted and you will experience setbacks along the way. But if you plan ahead and have realistic expectations, you *will* reach your goals.

OVERCOMING TEMPTATION

Have you ever been working toward a goal, or maybe you've achieved your goal, only to have something come along and knock you off course and put you right back where you started? When making lifestyle changes, such as losing weight or starting an exercise program, people report several situations that knock them off track. It's important to understand what kinds of things will make it difficult for you to achieve your goals. Do any of the following sound familiar to you?

- Stress and other emotional factors
- Illness or injury (to self or a loved one)
- Scheduling challenges
- Holidays and special occasions
- Influence of others
- Overwork
- Bad weather
- Travel and vacations

Once you understand how you are likely to be tempted and where your challenges are likely to come from, you can begin building a plan to prevent these situations from knocking you off course. When it comes to your health, happiness and quality of life, don't let guilt, negative thinking, embarrassment, feelings of failure, temporary setbacks or anything else come between you and your worthwhile goal. For encouragement, read Romans 8:28-39. Learn to view setbacks and slips as learning opportunities to help you grow stronger.

When it comes to making lifestyle changes, you *will* be tempted. Read the account of Eve's temptation in Genesis 3:1-6. Look at many of the ways in which she was tempted.

- **Spiritual:** "You will not surely die . . . you will be like God."
- **Emotional:** "The woman saw that the fruit of the tree was pleasing."
- **Intellectual:** "[The fruit also was] desirable for gaining wisdom."
- **Physical:** "She took some and ate it."
- **Social:** "She also gave some to her husband."

One of the best ways to overcome temptation is to rely on God's Word. Post Scripture (such as 1 Corinthians 10:13) in a prominent place to remind you that God will help you stay the course. He will provide a way out of temptation. If you are willing to act on what God provides, you can overcome temptation.

A LESSON ON LEARNING

When making lifestyle changes, it's important to learn from both your successes and your setbacks. Ask yourself if your expectations and feelings are realistic. Once you have set a worthwhile goal, be persistent about achieving success. When you are tempted or when you experience a setback, think about what went wrong. Focus on the positive and explore ways to prevent it from happening next time.

> The keys to successful lifestyle change are *staying on track* when times get tough and *bouncing back* after a setback.

SCRIPTURES TO HELP YOU
OVERCOME TEMPTATION

*No temptation has seized you except what is common to man.
And God is faithful; he will not let you be tempted beyond
what you can bear. But when you are tempted, he will also
provide a way out so that you can stand up under it.*

1 CORINTHIANS 10:13

*For we do not have a high priest who is unable to sympathize with
our weaknesses, but we have one who has been tempted in every way,
just as we are—yet was without sin. Let us then approach the throne
of grace with confidence, so that we may receive mercy
and find grace to help us in our time of need.*

HEBREWS 4:15-16

*We also rejoice in our sufferings, because we know that
suffering produces perseverance; perseverance, character;
and character, hope. And hope does not disappoint us,
because God has poured out his love into our hearts
by the Holy Spirit, whom he has given us.*

ROMANS 5:3-5

*Therefore, since we are surrounded by such a great cloud
of witnesses, let us throw off everything that hinders and
the sin that so easily entangles, and let us run with
perseverance the race marked out for us.*

HEBREWS 12:1

*I have hidden your word in my heart
that I might not sin against you.*

PSALM 119:11

Notes

1. David Dzewaltowki, cited in "Exercise Revolution—Do Something You Like to Do," Kansas State University, January 1997. http://www.k-state.edu/media/WEB/News/NewsReleases/list winterexercise.html (accessed October 2007).

2. "Lifelong Weight Management: Making the Leap to a Healthy Life," International Food Information Council Foundation, 1992. http://www.realtime.net/anr/weightmg.html (accessed October 2007).

3. Jeff Barge, "New Statistics: New Year's Resolution Usage Plummets from 88 percent to 45 percent—Are New Year's Resolutions a Thing of the Past?" data from telephone survey conducted by Stephen Shapiro, president of Goalfree.com, with the assistance of the Opinion Research Corporation of Princeton, New Jersey, December 13, 2005. http://www.welchmedia.com/news/article_385.shtml (accessed October 2007).

4. Susan Fiske, "Butt Out: Quit Smoking," *Psychology Today*, August 18, 2004. http://health.msn.com/guides/stopsmoking/articlepage.aspx?cp-documentid=100108050 (accessed October 2007).

letting others
help you succeed!

I t's important to find people who can help you achieve and maintain your goals and then get them involved to provide the support
and encouragement you need. Communication is the cornerstone
of any relationship, including your relationship with an accountability partner. Never expect your partner to read your mind. By
the same token, ask your partner how you can be a blessing in return.
Surprise him or her with rewards that show your appreciation. For a
partnership to be successful, each partner must both give and receive.

KINDS OF SUPPORT

Think about the types of support you need in your journey toward
health and who best fits that need.

- **Do you need someone to talk to?** Sometimes all you need is
  someone to listen. It's important to be able to share both
  positive and negative aspects of your life. With whom can
  you best share your feelings and experiences?

▪ **Do you need someone to participate with you?** It's often easier and more fun to make lifestyle changes when others are involved. Would your spouse or a friend go through the program with you? Who might want to exercise with you?

▪ **Do you need someone to provide encouragement?** A little motivation from a friend or loved one can go a long way. It's easy to get discouraged when you slip up or don't reach your goals as quickly as you would like. Who can help pick you up when you get down and discouraged? Who is a good encourager? Sometimes it's important to receive constructive criticism. Who can help you stay on task and push you when you need it? Ask others to give you the feedback you need—and be willing to accept what they say. Who is the best person to help you in this way?

▪ **Do you need someone to help with other aspects of your life?** Changing your lifestyle takes time and effort. Do you need help with personal responsibilities so that you can work out, attend a group meeting or cook a healthy meal? Who can help you around the house or at work so that you will have more time to make healthy changes in your life?

> **THE BUDDY SYSTEM**
>
> Is there someone who can either join you on your weight-loss journey or provide encouragement and honest feedback? Consider joining forces with a coworker or neighbor. You can commit to eating lunch together regularly—even sharing healthy snacks and meals. If time allows, you can work out together at lunch or at the end of the day. Talk about your successes and failures, and keep each other motivated. Making lifestyle changes with an accountability partner can make all the difference.

KEYS TO A SUCCESSFUL PARTNERSHIP

▪ **Set realistic goals.** Let family and friends know how important making a particular change is to you. Let them know that you are committed to success.

- **When asking for help, be as specific as you can.** Tell others exactly how they can help you. Better yet, work out a plan together and develop a contract.

- **Communicate openly and often about your thoughts, feelings and needs.** Practice positive communication—avoid being negative or critical.

- **Never expect one person to be all things for you.** Remember that only God can meet all of your needs.

- **Be sensitive to the needs of others.** Always consider how you can help those who help you. Don't hesitate to ask for the help you need, but try to offer something in return. Reward others for their help: Say thank you in a variety of ways.

overcoming
stress

WHAT STRESS IS

Do you ever feel as if life is stuck in high gear, and there's no way to slow it down? Do you want some down time but can't seem to find it amidst the pressures of work, home and other responsibilities?

If you identify with these questions, you're probably feeling the adverse effects of stress. Stress is our response to physical or emotional strain, such as overwork or too much worry.

God has given us the ability to recognize and respond to danger. Through the stress response, whose purpose is to protect us, our body responds to challenges by producing the hormones adrenaline and cortisol and releasing them into the bloodstream. These hormones speed up the heart rate, breathing rate, blood pressure and metabolism to prepare us for action. Stress experts call this the "fight or flight" response.

The stress response can help a person perform well under pressure. But experiencing long-term stress can create stress overload. When a person's body pumps out extra stress hormones over an extended period of time, he or she will feel depleted or overwhelmed. In fact, much of our stress is caused by thinking about things that haven't yet happened and probably never will. Over time, the stress response begins to take its toll on the body, mind and spirit.

THE HARMFUL EFFECTS OF STRESS

Some experts refer to stress as "hurry sickness." According to the American Psychological Association, two-thirds of office visits to family doctors are for stress-related symptoms.[1]

KICKING THE HABIT

A number of addictions can be linked to stress: overeating, smoking, drinking and drug abuse, to name a few. By eliminating or minimizing stress, you are more inclined to kick a bad habit.

Our bodies are clearly not designed for chronic stress. Stress is linked to heart disease, high blood pressure, obesity, depression and unhealthy habits. Stress causes headaches, backaches and digestive problems. Chronic stress suppresses the immune system and makes the body susceptible to a variety of illnesses. Stress can make you feel angry, irritable, afraid, excited or helpless. Stress makes it hard to sleep or relax, and leaves you feeling fatigued.

It's no wonder that God's Word repeatedly tells us not to worry or be anxious (see Matthew 6:25; John 14:27; Philippians 4:6-7).

To find out if you are stressed, answer each of the following questions:

- Do you often feel tense, nervous or anxious?
- Do you have a hard time relaxing or turning off your thoughts?
- Do you often worry about all the things you have to do?
- Do you have a hard time concentrating or staying focused?
- Do you often feel like things are out of your control?
- Do you constantly feel like you're in a hurry?
- Do you notice that you're irritable or get angry often?
- Do you often take on more than you can handle?

If you answered yes to one or more of these questions, chances are that stress is taking its toll on your health and quality of life. Are you ready to learn some ways to change your response to the challenges of your life?

A BIBLICAL PLAN FOR TAMING THE STRESS RESPONSE

Trust in God

"Trust in the LORD with all your heart and lean not on your own understanding; in all your ways acknowledge him, and he will make your paths straight" (Proverbs 3:5-6).

Do you view life from God's perspective? Have you gotten out of touch with God and His purpose for your life? Whose strength do you rely on when you're faced with a challenge or feeling overwhelmed? Stress is a signal to return your focus to God. So when you're feeling stressed, remember that God loves you and is in control of all things.

Overcome Stress Through Prayer

"Do not be anxious about anything, but in everything, by prayer and petition, with thanksgiving, present your requests to God. And the peace of God, which transcends all understanding, will guard your hearts and your minds in Christ Jesus" (Philippians 4:6-7).

What happens to your prayer life during times of stress? Never underestimate the power of prayer in dealing with the challenges of life. Learn to trust the Lord; He will provide a way through for you.

Take Positive Steps to Change the Situation

"Whatever you have learned or received or heard from me, or seen in me—put it into practice. And the God of peace will be with you" (Philippians 4:9).

The key to dealing with stress is to take positive action. Nothing is ever changed by worry. Identify the source of your stress and begin taking steps to deal with it from all angles.

Exercise is the best method for lowering cortisol levels that have risen in response to stress.

The Spiritual Angle: What does God's Word say? "Finally, brothers, whatever is true, whatever is noble, whatever is right, whatever is pure, whatever is lovely, whatever is admirable—if anything is excellent or praiseworthy—think about such things" (Philippians 4:8).

The Emotional Angle: Be purposeful about avoiding negative thoughts. A positive outlook will help you cope better with stressful situations.

The Intellectual Angle: Focus your mind on the truth. Think about the source or causes of your stress, and seek successful solutions.

The Physical Angle: Strive to eat healthfully and exercise 30 minutes a day, a proven stress-buster.

The Social Angle: Get to know your First Place 4 Health family. Finding a support group for information, encouragement and fun will help relieve stress.

Note

1. "Stress," Pharmasave Library Statistics, citing an American Psychological Association study in 2005. http://content.nhiondemand.com/psv/HC2.asp?objID=100248&cType=hc (accessed October 2007).

how to
H.A.L.T. defeat!

Dear friends, I urge you, as aliens and strangers
in the world, to abstain from sinful desires,
which war against your soul.

1 PETER 2:11

We can't separate the physical from the spiritual. We are called to love the Lord with our entire being and do all things for His honor and glory. That means we need to stop doing things that keep us in defeat and despair when it comes to losing weight and maintaining a healthy, fit-for-service body that brings glory to God. This is another way of saying, "abstain from the desires that war against your soul."

The word "stop" has many synonyms, but there is one synonym that has particular application for our efforts: HALT. Not only does the word "halt" mean to stop, but it also can be turned into an acrostic that gives us some practical tips to rise from defeat when it comes to losing weight and maintaining a healthy lifestyle. The acrostic H.A.L.T. invites us to say STOP! before we become too . . .

Hungry

Anxious

Lonely

Tired

Just as soon as any of those feelings begins to surface, stop whatever you're doing and ask yourself what you need to do so that your unmet needs don't turn into an occasion for out-of-control eating. It's not your need that is sinful—trying to satisfy a legitimate need in an illegitimate way wages war against your soul and puts those extra pounds and inches on your body.

Which of the feelings spelled out in the acrostic H.A.L.T.—hunger, anxiety, loneliness, tiredness—are stopped by the action steps listed below? Consider these actions as the foundational steps that will walk you toward your goal of a healthy lifestyle:

- Show up at your weekly First Place 4 Health meeting
- Stay in touch with your accountability partner
- Eat healthfully
- Encourage others
- Pray
- Commit your worries to God
- Read your Bible daily
- Study your Bible (beginning with your First Place 4 Health Bible study)
- Memorize Scripture
- Use your Live It Tracker to record your success
- Exercise (programmed or lifestyle activity) at least 30 minutes a day

Now think of ways that you can use some of the action steps above to apply the H.A.L.T. acrostic to your life today. Stop doing those things that war against your mind, emotions, body and spirit!

relapse prevention

We are not unaware of Satan's schemes.

2 CORINTHIANS 2:11

The *American Heritage Dictionary* defines "relapse" as follows: "To fall or slide back into a former state . . . to regress after partial recovery . . . to slip back into bad ways; backslide."[1] Most of us are way too familiar with the "three steps forward, two steps back" process of trying to learn new behavior. But when it comes to our First Place 4 Health efforts, falling back into old habit patterns is not inevitable. There are things we can do to make slow, steady progress without falling into old ruts that keep us in defeat.

One simple battle tactic that leads to success is to *starve sin*. Much like ancient warriors used to surround an enemy city so that the inhabitants did not have access to food and water, we need to sever the supply lines that feed our old habits.

We begin this "starving sin" process by learning to recognize our vulnerability, to accept it and to avoid situations and places—those slippery slopes—that set us up for failure. This may mean completely avoiding certain people, places and things because of the magnetic pull their influence exerts over us.

Often what lures you away from your resolve is not even food, so look for a pattern in the way Satan tempts you. What you will find is usually the same time, same place, same companions, same circumstances, over and over again. If you find that certain situations continually undermine your resolve and contribute to your drinking, overeating, impulse buying, gossiping or whatever else gratifies your sinful nature, then those are situations you must eliminate if you are going to stand strong against the wiles of the evil one.

All change begins with awareness. Spend some time today identifying the people, places and situations that easily lead you back into old habit patterns, and list them below.

1 _____

2 _____

3 _____

After you have identified the areas in which you are most vulnerable to temptation, determine not to be self-indulgent. The apostle Paul put it this way: "Do not think about how to gratify the desires of the sinful nature" (Romans 13:14). Satan knows our weaknesses and uses all the tools at his command to constantly keep us in spiritual jeopardy. When we are aware of our weaknesses, we can avoid what causes us to fall back into old behavior. We can exercise self-control—one of the fruit of the Spirit—if we choose to let Him develop it in us.

If you hope to eliminate old behavior, you simply must eliminate the things that allow it to flourish.

Perhaps you need to rehearse saying no when your eating buddies ask you to join them for a meal. Maybe you need to practice not buying the food that leads you to a binge or not working through your lunch hour so that at 4:00 P.M. you are ready to devour anything in sight! If ice cream is your weakness, find a new way home that doesn't take you past the ice cream store. Choose the grocery store checkout aisle without candy. List three specific measures you will put into action this week as you begin to starve sin:

1 _____

2 _____

3 _____

When you have your plan in place, use the words "STOP IT!" whenever you find yourself opening up those old supply lines that feed the enemy. Until we learn to starve sin, we will continue to gratify our sinful nature. We are not on a diet; we are learning to starve sin by cutting off the enemy's supply route so that we can give Christ first place in our life.

Note

1. "Relapse," Dictionary.com, *The American Heritage® Dictionary of the English Language, Fourth Edition* (New York: Houghton Mifflin Company, 2004). http://dictionary.reference.com/browse/relapse (accessed October 2007).

Spiritual Well-Being

the faith factor

N umerous studies have indicated a connection between healing and prayer. It has been reported that 82 percent of Americans believe that prayer can cure serious illness, and 64 percent want their physicians to pray with them.[1] Faith and prayer are good for the body, mind and soul. Recent research suggests that faith is an important factor in the prevention of disease and the promotion of health. In addition, numerous studies show that religious commitment is beneficial to health and well-being:

- In 2001, the *British Medical Journal* reported a randomized study of the effects of prayer on patients with bloodstream infections that demonstrated that the patients who received prayer had a statistically significant shorter hospital stay and a more rapid recovery (shorter duration of fever) than the group that did not receive prayer.[2]

- A study published in the *Journal of the American Medical Association* looked at factors considered important at the end of life. In a random sampling of 340 patients with advanced illnesses, researchers found that "being at peace with God" was ranked No. 2 in importance, just slightly lower than pain control.[3]

- In a study conducted by the University of California at Berkeley, researchers followed 5,286 men and women over a period of 28 years and found that those who frequently attended religious services lived longer than those who did not. They also were more likely to quit smoking, increase exercise, increase social contacts and have better marriages.[4]

- Another study found that people who attend church regularly have 50 percent less risk of dying from heart disease and 56 percent less risk of dying from lung disease compared to those who rarely go to church. They also had 74 percent less risk of dying from liver disease and 53 percent less risk of dying from suicide.[5]

RELIGION AND DEPRESSION

A recent Duke University study involving 1,000 patients with major and minor depression showed that the severity of depression was associated with lower religious attendance, less prayer and less Scripture reading.[7]

- Research shows that faith has beneficial effects on blood pressure. A study of more than 4,000 people ages 65 and older found that those who attended religious services at least once a week and prayed or studied the Bible at least daily had consistently lower blood pressure than those who did so less frequently or not at all.[6]

Here are some important questions to ask yourself:

1. Do I understand that good health requires balance in all areas of my life?
2. Am I willing to open myself up to the spiritual support of others?
3. How does my faith influence my daily habits and choices?

A strong faith and regular prayer do not guarantee that you will live a long life or be free from disease; they simply lower your risk. It's important to understand that emotional stress and physical illness are not forms of divine punishment. God loves you and desires the very best for you (see Romans 8:31-32), but your daily choices have a strong influence on your overall health and well-being. That's why your personal faith can be a strong motivator for healthy and purposeful living.

Notes

1. Ann Ameling, RN, MSN, "Prayer: An Ancient Healing Practice Becomes New Again," *Holistic Nursing Practice*, 2000, 14(3):40-48.

2. Leonard Leibovici, "Beyond Science? Effects of Remote, Retroactive Intercessory Prayer on Outcomes in Patients with Bloodstream Infection: Randomized Controlled Trial," *British Medical Journal*. December 22-29, 2001, 323:1450-1451.

3. K. E. Steinhauser, N. A. Christakis, E. C. Clipp, et al, "Factors Considered Important at the End of Life by Patients, Family, Physicians and Other Care Providers," *Journal of the American Medical Association*, 284:2476-2482.

4. W. J. Strawbridge, R. D. Cohen, S. J. Shema and G. A. Kaplan, "Frequent Attendance at Religious Services and Mortality over 28 Years," *American Journal of Public Health*, 1997, 87(6):957-961. http://www.ncbi.nlm.nih.gov/sites/entrez?cmd=Retrieve&db=pubmed&dopt=AbstractPlus&list_uids=9224176 (accessed October 2007).

5. H. G. Koenig, L. K. George, J. C. Hays, et al, "The Relationship Between Religious Activities and Blood Pressure in Older Adults," *International Journal of Psychology in Medicine*, 1998, 28(2):189-213.

6. Ibid.

7. H. G. Koenig, "Religion and Depression in Older Medical Inpatients," *American Journal of Geriatric Psychiatry*, 15:282-291, April 2007. http://ajgponline.org/cgi/content/abstract/15/4/282 (accessed October 2007).

making time for Bible study and prayer

Your relationship with God is the foundation for your spiritual growth. The Great Commandment (see Mark 12:28-31) calls you into relationship with Him. Christ is the One for whom you were created (see Colossians 1:15-20), and it is He who gives you strength (see Philippians 4:13).

Like any other relationship, your relationship with God takes time and commitment to develop. The time you spend in prayer and in God's Word, the Bible, will help you develop intimacy with God and deepen your relationship with Him.

Daily devotions (a quiet time to meet with God) and prayer are lifelines in a hectic world, especially when we're trying to make lifestyle changes. In the midst of the whirlwind, we can hear Jesus say, "Come away to a quiet place, My child, and rest for a while." He spoke similar words to His disciples (see Matthew 11:28); He beckons you to do the same. Your Savior calls you to spend time with Him. It's the very best use of your time!

YOUR APPOINTMENT WITH GOD

Having a quiet time with God is a discipline that must be developed through practice. Deep relationships are always intentional. They require time and effort.

There are no rules regarding when to do your quiet time, so choose a time that works best for you. Find times and places that will allow you to give the Lord your undivided attention. Perhaps that's in the morning before everyone gets up. It may be in the evening after the children are in bed. Maybe noon is a time when you can get away to be with the Lord.

How much time do you have to spend on devotions? Once you've decided on the best time, write it down on your calendar or in your daily planner to establish a routine. Just as with exercise and other lifestyle changes, many people try to do too much too soon. Set aside an amount of time that works for you. Adjust your schedule as you learn what works best.

Commune with God

Take some time to learn how you best communicate with God and listen to His voice. This may be different on different days or at different times of the day. Learn what works best for you.

- **How do you best communicate with God?** Whether through writing, talking, singing or playing music, meditating or other methods, try a variety of ways to spend time with Him.

- **Where is your favorite place to meet with God?** When you spend time with God, you need to be able to relax and focus your attention on Him. It's important to find a special place where you're comfortable. In Matthew 6:6, Jesus said, "When you pray, go into your room, close the door and pray to your Father, who is unseen. Then your Father, who sees what is done in secret, will reward you."

Study God's Word

There are lots of great ways to study and meditate on God's Word. For variety, consider the following:

- Use a daily devotional book as your guide.
- Use a Bible with study notes or other references.

- Follow one of the systematic plans for reading through the Bible. (You may want to consider reading a one-year Bible— ask at your local Christian bookstore.)
- Meditate on and study a favorite verse, passage of Scripture or hymn.
- Get involved in a study group or with an accountability partner and study together; establish a reading or daily devotions schedule.
- If you have a long commute to work, listening to the Bible on cassette, CD or MP3 is an excellent way to spend quality time with the Lord.
- You will probably develop other creative ideas as you continue to study.

Get prepared by gathering materials ahead of time, and keep them in a specific place. Or if you like to move around, keep your Bible study materials in a basket, box or other container so that you can keep everything together. In addition to a Bible, notebook and pen or pencil, consider adding a Bible dictionary, additional Bible translations, a hymnal or songbook, a journal, a devotional book and anything else that you might find helpful. These resources can add variety to your quiet time; having them easily available will encourage you to spend more time studying and praying.

Use a Prayer List

Organizing a prayer list can help you focus your prayers on issues that are most important. When your mind wanders, use your list to get your mind focused. Write down the important

> **MAKING PRAYER A PRIORITY**
>
> Discipline is the key to establishing a strong prayer life. Philip Yancey, author of a book on prayer, says, "Much of the benefit of prayer comes as a result of consistency, the simple act of showing up. . . . Many days I would be hard-pressed to describe a direct benefit. I keep on, though, whether it feels like I am profiting or not. I show up in hopes of getting to know God better, and perhaps hearing from God in ways accessible only through quiet and solitude."[1]

issues and concerns in your life. Keep an ongoing list of people who need prayer. Other areas for prayer might include world issues, government leaders, missionaries and ministries. Writing down when those prayers were answered is a great encouragement to continue to pray.

Keep a Journal

Keeping a spiritual journal is a concrete way to keep in touch with God and what's going on in your life. Keep a record of prayer requests, answered prayers and other ways God is working in your life and the lives of those around you. As time goes on, you will have a memorial of your journey with Him. Journals help to personalize your devotional time and keep you motivated.

OVERCOME ROADBLOCKS

Like any discipline, obstacles and roadblocks come up to prevent your having a quiet time as part of your daily routine. Do any of these excuses sound familiar?

- I don't know where to begin.
- I don't know how or what to pray.
- I don't have time.
- I can't seem to keep myself motivated.
- The Bible is confusing to me sometimes.

What are your barriers to quiet time and prayer? How can you overcome them? Talk about your needs and brainstorm solutions with family, friends or a Bible study group. Do not forget that quiet time is a discipline to be developed; give yourself time to learn and grow. Even when you don't feel like it, make it a priority to get into the Word and spend some time with your heavenly Father. You'll be glad you did.

Note

1. Philip Yancey, *Prayer: Does It Make Any Difference?* (Grand Rapids, MI: Zondervan, 2006), pp. 165-166.

steps for spiritual growth!

The following are some practical steps that you can take that will aid you in your spiritual growth:

Prayer
- Prayer provides spiritual food and water for daily living.
- Prayer helps you give your life back to God daily.
- Prayer allows you to confess your sins daily.

> *If we confess our sins, he is faithful and just and will forgive us our sins and purify us from all unrighteousness* (1 John 1:9).

The Bible
- Studying the Bible keeps you grounded in the essential ingredients for daily living.
- The Bible teaches you about the life of Jesus (read the New Testament Gospels of Matthew, Mark, Luke and John).
- The Bible assures you of your salvation.

> *I write these things to you who believe in the name of the Son of God so that you may know that you have eternal life* (1 John 5:13).

The Church

- The Church provides fellowship with other believers in addition to a place to worship God.
- Being baptized is the first step to obedience (see Matthew 3:13-17, which tells of Jesus' baptism).
- Become a member of a Bible-teaching, Bible-believing community of believers.
- The Church is Christ's Body on Earth, formed to spread the Good News of Jesus' life, death and resurrection.

So in Christ we who are many form one body, and each member belongs to all the others (Romans 12:5).

Sharing Your Faith

- Jesus commanded us to share with others what Christ has done and how He continues to work in our lives.

Then Jesus came to them and said, "All authority in heaven and on earth has been given to me. Therefore go and make disciples of all nations, baptizing them in the name of the Father and of the Son and of the Holy Spirit, and teaching them to obey everything I have commanded you. And surely I am with you always, to the very end of the age" (Matthew 28:18-20).

- Sharing your faith with others is telling your story—how God has changed you and how He helps you daily.

Do not worry about how you will defend yourselves or what you will say, for the Holy Spirit will teach you at that time what you should say (Luke 12:11-12).

● The Bible promises that the Holy Spirit will help you.

But you will receive power when the Holy Spirit comes on you; and you will be my witnesses in Jerusalem, and in all Judea and Samaria, and to the ends of the earth (Acts 1:8).

Note

1. Nelson Price, "Synonym for Church," SermonSearch.com, August 9, 1993. http://www.ser monsearch.com/content.aspx?id=12796 (accessed September 2007).

accepting God's gracious invitation !

If anyone would come after me,
he must deny himself and take up
his cross daily and follow me.

LUKE 9:23

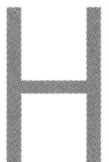enry Blackaby, in his classic book *Experiencing God*, lists seven essential truths for those of us who strive to give Christ first place in our lives:

1 God is always at work around you.

2 God pursues a continuing love relationship with you that is real and personal.

3 God invites you to become involved with Him in His work.

4 God speaks by the Holy Spirit through the Bible, prayer, circumstances and the Church to reveal Himself, His purposes and His ways.

5 God's invitation for you to work with Him always leads you to a crisis of belief that requires faith and action.

6 You must make major adjustments in your life to join God in what He is doing.

7 You come to know God by experience as you obey Him and He accomplishes His work through you.[1]

We have a tendency to look around, searching for the work God is calling us to do, and feeling frustrated when the answers we seek don't come. Clarity arrives when we finally realize that God is calling us to start by joining Him in the renewal of our own lives. God is in the business of renovation and restoration, and His first project is renewing those who are called to help Him carry the Good News to a lost and dying world. Reread Henry Blackaby's statements and let the truth of those words sink in: *God is at work in your life, and He is inviting you to join Him in this exciting work!*

You can expect that God's invitation will lead to a crisis of belief that requires faith and action—you will be called to make major adjustments in your life if you are going to join God in what He is doing.

As you begin your First Place 4 Health journey, spend a few minutes asking yourself these questions:

- What is God doing in my life right now that requires my cooperation?
- How is God speaking to me through the First Place 4 Health program?
- When I accept God's invitation, I can expect a crisis of belief that will require faith and action. Am I prepared to face that crisis and respond in faith and action?
- What do I need to stop doing so that I can accept God's invitation, obey His clear directions and allow Him to mold me into a vessel fit for service according to His plan and purpose for my life?

God is calling you to respond to Him in faith, action, love and obedience. Are you ready to join Him in His work? It's not about special diets or weighing and measuring food. It's not about how long you exercise each day, or checking off boxes on your Live It Tracker (see your *Member's Guide*). These are merely tools to help you achieve the ultimate goal: a personal, loving, intimate and interactive relationship with the Risen Savior who invites you to care for yourself because He cares for you! Anything you do—or fail to do—that hinders that relationship wages war against your soul. Neglecting to care for yourself and making choices that do damage to your body, the temple of God's Holy Spirit, are two of those things. What do you need to stop doing today so that you can present your body as a living sacrifice to the One who gave His life that you might be right with God?

We have a tendency to look around, searching for the work God is calling us to do, and feeling frustrated when the answers we seek don't come. Clarity arrives when we finally realize that God is calling us to start by joining Him in the renewal of our own lives.

restoration and forgiveness

Forgive as the Lord forgave you.

COLOSSIANS 3:13

Above all else, guard your heart, for it is the wellspring of life.

PROVERBS 4:23

A paradox is a statement that appears to contradict itself but is really a truth applied to a deeper level of our being. Paradoxes may seem confusing when we try to interpret spiritual truth based on physical reality. This is certainly the case when we consider how God commands us both to forgive and to establish healthy boundaries that keep us from being exposed to further harm. Scripture tells us to forgive those who have offended us (see Colossians 3:13) *and* to protect ourselves from future abuse (see Proverbs 4:23).

Those of us who have been the object of abuse are often hesitant to forgive our abusers because we fear forgiveness will open us up to future harm. But without appropriate boundaries, forgiving or not forgiving someone will not affect the outcome. Only proper boundaries can prevent continued abuse, and forgiveness is a necessary step toward establishing healthy boundaries.

Make a list of people who have injured you and write each name in a space below. To the right of each name write a short statement explaining how allowing that person back in your personal space might put you, or those entrusted to your care, in jeopardy.

NAME	RISK OF FUTURE HARM

Perhaps you're thinking, *I'm told to forgive these people, but they are a threat to my spiritual, emotional, mental or physical security. Can that be what God wants for me?* The key to understanding this paradox is to understand the difference between forgiveness and restored relationships.

Forgiveness means giving up our right to get even, and leaving vengeance to God (see Romans 12:19). Forgiveness is a unilateral decision that does not require the involvement of the other person. We choose to untie ourselves from past hurts rather than allow them to poison the present and the future. Forgiveness is not dependent on the offender's response. As Christ's followers, we forgive so that we can worship God unhindered by toxins that pollute what God has redeemed and called holy—*us!*

Forgiveness gives us the freedom to set boundaries because it unhooks us from the hurtful person and allows us to act responsibly and wisely. Until we forgive, we are still tied to a destructive relationship. Lack of forgiveness destroys boundaries; forgiveness creates them.

Restored relationships require both parties' involvement: One repents of the offense(s) and the other person forgives the offense(s). Take a moment to read Luke 3:8-14. Repentance is not about idle words. For restoration to take place, the offending party's repentance must manifest itself in changed behavior. The fruit of repentance does not include continued abuse.

God calls us to forgive as He has forgiven us, but He also admonishes us not to open ourselves up to further abuse. Damaged relationships can be restored in trust and safety only when both parties accept mutual responsibility to each other and to the relationship. Our Lord calls us to set limits to guard our physical, mental, emotional and spiritual "property" until the one who has violated our boundaries has repented and can be trusted again.

We need to associate with like-minded individuals who are willing to admit when they do something that causes us harm. We also need to be aware and acknowledge when we hurt others. We learn through failure, so when we own up to our shortcomings, amend our behavior and strive to change, we experience a growth spurt. As Christians, we can forgive each other over and over again and treat each other with dignity and respect, because both parties are committed to change and growth. With God's help, we can work through the problem together, restore the broken relationship and grow in the process.

Write about a time when confession and repentance allowed you to safely restore your relationship with someone who offended you.

_____

_____

_____

_____

How did you grow in your Christian walk as a result of that experience?

_____

_____

_____

_____

On the other hand, we need to avoid people who deny that they have hurt us, who find various ways to justify their unacceptable behavior or who have no desire to treat us with love, respect and dignity. A relationship with this type of person is destructive for all parties involved, and we must keep them at a safe distance. In extreme cases, we must avoid them altogether. Even though we have forgiven them, we do not need to allow them into our personal space.

When we stop expecting to have a healthy relationship with an unhealthy person, we are free to establish relationships that nourish and support our Christian maturity. This newfound freedom makes room for healthy relationships that contribute to our growth and healing. Take time today to assess the quality of your relationships by answering the following questions:

- Is there someone in your life with whom you continue to associate who repeatedly intrudes into your personal space and defiles what God has called you to keep holy and set apart for Him?
- Is there someone in your life who frequently shatters your plans and dreams?
- Is there someone in your life who sabotages your goals and tries to impose his or her thoughts and emotions on you?
- Is there someone in your life who promises to change but doesn't?

If you answered yes to any of these questions, you need to forgive that person and then post a *No Trespassing* sign on the gate of your heart. Remember, we are not to put God to the test by allowing abusive people into our personal space. God empowers us as we seek to obey His commands.

What action do you need to take today to forgive those who have hurt you and to take responsible action to protect your heart?

_____

_____

_____

_____

Write a prayer in your journal asking God to help you establish relationships founded on mutual respect and responsibility and to help you build healthy boundaries to protect you from those who continue to do you harm.

the lordship
of Christ

Why do you call me Lord, Lord, and do not do what I say?

LUKE 6:46

What does it mean to surrender to Christ's Lordship in every aspect of life and put this decision into practice by daily self-discipline? Jesus asked His followers the piercing question, "Why do you call me Lord, Lord, and do not do what I say?" (Luke 6:46). That question is directed at us as well. Are we calling Jesus "Lord, Lord," and claiming that He has the number-one spot in our life while engaging in behavior that is displeasing to Him?

It's one thing to say Jesus is Lord; it is another thing to put those words into action. The following Scripture passages tell us what Jesus' Lordship means in our life:

- Submission to God's will (see Matthew 8:2)
- Placing God first (see Matthew 22:36-40)
- Accepting responsibility and accountability (see Matthew 25:14-30)

- Doing God's will (see Matthew 7:21-27)
- Obedience, regardless of the cost (see John 21:15-23)

It has been said that there are three classes of people when it comes to the Lordship of Christ. Prayerfully consider the verses you have just read and circle the choice below that best describes where you are in regard to surrendering to the Lordship of Christ. If you are in between two of the verses, you can place an X between the numbers.

1. Those who neither call Him Lord nor do the things He says

2. Those who call Him Lord but do not do the things He says

3. Those who call Him Lord and do the things He says

Why did you choose that statement?

_____

_____

_____

_____

_____

Lordship is the pivotal point of the Christian life. The choices we make every day prove the truth or hypocrisy of our words. Lordship is also a journey, beginning in spiritual infancy and finding its fullness in the mature Christian life. One way to visualize this journey is to see it as a ladder.

> It is one thing to say Jesus is Lord; it is another to put those words into action.

Study the Scripture across from each description and then mark where you are on the Lordship Ladder.

Consider what you can stop doing, using the words "Stop It!" whenever needed, so that you can climb to the next rung as you move toward the peace and joy promised to all who make Jesus Christ the Lord of all.

THE LORDSHIP LADDER

Peace	Galatians 2:20
Total surrender	Romans 12:1-2
Hunger for righteousness	Matthew 5:6
Partial surrender	Luke 9:57-62
Wrestling	Romans 7:19-20
Seeking	Isaiah 55:6-7
Instability	James 1:8

What action will you take today to make your words reality?

Section Three

Mental Well-Being

you are
unique !

Do you not know that your body is a temple of the Holy Spirit,
who is in you, whom you have received from God?

1 CORINTHIANS 6:19

A healthy self-image is an important part of being a new creation in Christ. When you begin to understand what Christ has done for you, your self-talk will begin to change. Let's explore some steps that will help you realize who you truly are in Christ.

STEP 1: UNDERSTAND THAT YOU ARE UNIQUE

It's a proven fact: There is no one else exactly like you! You are uniquely created to be one of a kind. Nothing about you is a mistake. Read the psalmist's words regarding your individuality:

You created my inmost being; you knit me together in my mother's womb. I praise you because I am fearfully and wonderfully made;

your works are wonderful, I know that full well. My frame was not hidden from you when I was made in the secret place. When I was woven together in the depths of the earth, your eyes saw my un-formed body. All the days ordained for me were written in your book before one of them came to be (Psalm 139:13-16).

Identify something unique about yourself that sets you apart from others and that you can offer to God for His service.

Spend a few moments in prayer thanking God for your unique design and for His intimate involvement in creating you.

STEP 2: THINK ABOUT WHAT IS TRUE

Another area in which people have many faulty assumptions is their appearance. Take a look at the following faulty assumptions and truths to ponder.

Faulty Assumption—Looks are central to who I am.
Truth to Ponder—Consider the lives of people such as Corrie ten Boom, Billy Graham and Mother Teresa. Their looks are not the first thing you think of when you admire them.

Faulty Assumption—The first things people notice about my appearance are my imperfections.
Truth to Ponder—Most people notice your best feature first. Remember, we're harder on ourselves than other people are!

Faulty Assumption—Appearance always reflects the inner person.
Truth to Ponder—Consider Christ. Scripture tells us that there was nothing lovely about His appearance that would draw us to Him (see Isaiah 53:2).

The next two "Truths to Ponder" have been left blank for you to complete.

Faulty Assumption—My appearance is responsible for much of what has happened to me.

Truth to Ponder— _____

_____

_____

_____

_____

_____

Faulty Assumption—The only way I can ever be happy is to change the way I look.

Truth to Ponder— _____

_____

_____

_____

_____

_____

STEP 3: SEE YOUR BODY AS A GIFT

Do a little experiment. Close your eyes and picture yourself. Now suppose you were given the opportunity to ask God to change one thing about your body—what would you ask Him to change?

Now identify at least one thing about your physical body that you really like—not your personality or something inside you, but about your body. Was that easy or difficult?

Ask God to begin changing your thoughts about your body. Ask Him to instill in you a sense of wonder for how intricately complex and amazing He has created your body to interact with your brain. You are fearfully and wonderfully made!

a healthy body image!

When we pick up any fashion magazine, flip on the TV or notice the billboards lining the roadway, what do we see? Everywhere we turn, we're presented with unrealistic images of how we should look, what we should wear and how we should live. Beautiful bodies are placed alongside ads for fattening foods, sending the message that you *can* have it all. How do you measure up to what you see? How do these images and messages influence the way you feel about yourself? Do they influence your lifestyle habits and the goals you set for yourself? Are these messages and ideals in line with God's purpose for your life?

Don't let the media or society's unrealistic expectations influence the goals you set or the way you feel about yourself. Trying to live up to these unrealistic demands will only lead to failure, guilt and disappointment. Set your sights on the more important things in life: your relationship to God, good health and effective living.

Achieving the current ideal body image requires extremes of diet, exercise and cosmetic surgery; it's an image that often comes at the price of good health. Despite what we're led to believe, our society's version of the ideal body is outside the reach of the majority of men and women and is not a matter of self-discipline. There's absolutely no truth to the prevailing message that thinness equals health and happiness.

WHAT THE NUMBERS SHOW

- According to the North American Association for the Study of Obesity, 52 percent of men and 66 percent of women in America are unhappy with their weight. Studies show that 80 percent of women are dissatisfied with their appearance at one time or another.[1]

- It is estimated that 40 to 50 percent of women are trying to lose weight at any given time. Many women on diets are already at or below a normal body weight.[2]

- In 2000, 79 percent of Americans reported they were trying to lose weight through dieting. However, most were not incorporating recommended weight-loss strategies.[3]

- Twenty years ago, fashion models weighed 8 percent less than the average woman; today they weigh 23 percent less. The average woman is 5'4" and weighs nearly 145 pounds, while the average fashion model is 5'9" and weighs 110 pounds.[4]

- Eating disorders are on the rise—in both women and men![5]

Having a positive attitude and accepting who you are is the first step to making healthy lifestyle changes. It is actually much easier to make permanent lifestyle changes once you accept the reality that you may never have a perfect body shape; the goal is good health and better living. Take a moment to consider your reasons for wanting to lose weight.

A REDEFINITION OF "IDEAL"

You should primarily judge your success by how well you meet your goals for good health. Rather than focusing on the scale, set your sights on healthy eating habits and regular physical activity. If you are overweight, healthy lifestyle changes that result in a 10 percent weight loss will result in significant improvements in your health and quality of life, but may not be enough to achieve your *ideal* body weight. The goal is not to have a perfect model's figure but to live a healthier, happier and more productive life—in the body that you have! These are achievable goals.

"If shop mannequins were real women, they'd be too thin to menstruate."
—Stephanie Marston, *If Not Now, When?*[6]

There's a popular quote that goes something like this: "Your body is where you will spend the rest of your life; isn't it about time you made it your home?" Actually, isn't it about time you made it God's home, too (see 1 Corinthians 6:19-20)?

Notes

1. C. M. Shisslak, M. Crago, K. M. McKnight, et al, "Potential Risk Factors Associated with Weight Control Behaviors in Elementary and Middle School Girls," *Journal of Psychosomatic Research,* March-April 1998, 44(3-4):301-13.
2. C. L. Bish, H. M. Blanck, M. K. Serdula, et al, "Diet and Physical Activity Behaviors Among Americans Trying to Lose Weight: 2000 Behavioral Risk Factor Surveillance System," *Obesity Research*, March 2005, 13(3):596-607.
3. M. K. Serdula, A. H. Mokdad, D. F. Williamson, et al, "Prevalence of Attempting Weight Loss and Strategies for Controlling Weight," *JAMA,* 1999, 282:1353-1358.
4. Debra L. Gimlin, *Body Work: Beauty and Self-Image in American Culture* (Berkeley, CA: University of California Press, 2002).
5. C. G. Fairburn and Z. Cooper, "Thinking Afresh About the Classification of Eating Disorders," *International Journal of Eating Disorders,* November 2007, 40(S3):S107-S110.
6. Stephanie Marston, *If Not Now, When? Reclaiming Ourselves at Midlife* (New York: Grand Central Publishing, 2002).

healthy living
on the job !

Whether you work in the home, work from home or work outside of the home, work is a necessary part of life. It can provide both joy and satisfaction. Unfortunately, it also brings schedules, deadlines, long hours and many other responsibilities and stresses.

Those who work in the home or from home have unique challenges in the area of accountability. They have more ease in food preparation but more opportunity to get off track because they don't have other people around during their workday. They may be more tempted to "graze" on snacks throughout the day, especially if they are by themselves. Solutions for the person who works alone lie mostly in a consistent record of food intake and exercise. He or she should also check in with an accountability partner by phone on a regular basis, especially when tempted to give in to the urge to get off track with food.

If you work outside of the home, your challenges will be more in the areas of planning ahead with food choices and how to get in some exercise. Prayerfully consider ways to make healthy living a part of each day. Here are some suggestions and tips to help you get started. Don't try to change everything at once. Start with the changes you're most ready to make and most confident will stick.

EAT HEALTHY

- **Never skip meals.** Your body needs food throughout the day for energy. Start your day with a nutritious breakfast and don't skip lunch. Every meal you miss robs your body of important nutrients. Skipping meals will make it more likely that you'll overeat later.

- **Prepare and take your own food.** You're much more likely to eat healthy meals and snacks if you prepare them yourself. The key is planning ahead.

- **Healthy eating at work begins at the grocery store.** Make a list of foods you enjoy that are easy to take to work. Choose fresh, canned or dried fruits; raw or canned vegetables; lean sandwich meats; low-fat crackers; bean- or broth-based soups; low-fat milk and yogurt.

- **Cook extra portions** with evening meals and pack the leftovers for work: homemade fast-food!

- **If you don't have a refrigerator at work, bring an ice cooler or insulated lunch bag.** Buy plastic containers in which you can store foods and beverages.

- **Store healthy snacks in your desk drawer, briefcase or car.** Low-fat crackers, graham crackers, cookies, bagels, fresh or dried fruit, cereal, popcorn and instant oatmeal are all great choices.

- **When eating out, choose restaurants and menu items carefully.** Don't be afraid to ask your server or chef specific questions about substitutions, ingredients or cooking methods.

- **Watch portion sizes;** the quantity served is usually much more than you need. Split your meal with a companion or save half for later.

- **Avoid fried foods and dishes cooked with heavy sauces or lots of cheese.** Choose bean- or broth-based soups, baked or grilled chicken, fresh salads with low-fat dressing, steamed vegetables, sandwiches with lean meat and fresh fruit.

- **Find two or three restaurants where you can make healthy choices;** recommend these places to your lunch partner when eating out.

BE MORE PHYSICALLY ACTIVE

Add physical activity to your workday whenever you can. Even 10 minutes of activity at a time, done throughout the day, can improve your health and fitness.

A study in the *Journal of Occupational and Environmental Medicine* showed that workers who are moderately active get along better with their coworkers and take fewer sick days than their inactive counterparts. Highly fit employees perform more work than their colleagues—with little effort.[1]

- Schedule physical activity just like you do important meetings.
- Park your car farther away from your office building.
- Take the stairs instead of the elevator.
- Use the bathroom on the next floor up or across the building.
- Deliver messages in person when possible.
- Take 10- to 15-minute walking breaks during your day.

- Stand up and do some stretching while you're talking on the phone.
- Buy some handheld weights or elastic exercise bands to use in your office.
- Go for a walk during your lunch hour.
- Start a walking group or exercise class at work.
- Make time for physical activity when you travel—walk in the airport between flights.
- Talk to your company about purchasing a few pieces of exercise equipment or implementing a wellness program. (Do your research about the benefits before making your request.)

REDUCE STRESS

You may not be able to eliminate the stress of your job, but you can learn to handle it in more positive ways. Stress often begins before you arrive at work: running late, taking care of personal responsibilities and fighting traffic. Here are some tips to help you reduce stress and respond more positively to the stress you may experience on the job.

- Get organized; do most of your preparation the night before.
- Be sure to get enough sleep. Most people need seven to nine hours of sleep every night. Discover how much sleep you need and try to get it every night.
- Try to arrange your schedule so that you can avoid driving in heavy traffic.
- Leave your home early enough so that you're not rushed.

A SOOTHING BEDTIME ROUTINE

Try establishing a relaxing nightly ritual. For instance, take a warm bath or read an uplifting devotional before you turn out the light. What kind of routine helps you wind down at night?

- Take time to relax before you leave for work or while you're in the car: breathe deeply, relax your muscles, pray or listen to relaxing music or an inspirational message.
- At work, take 10 to 15 minutes once or twice a day to relax and organize the rest of your day.
- Prioritize your daily and weekly activities.
- Learn to recognize things that are less important or not important at all, and don't waste your time and energy on them.
- Schedule time for your own needs.
- Focus on one thing at a time.
- Learn to say "No" or "I need help."
- Personalize your workspace with pictures and special messages.
- Avoid cigarette smoke and limit caffeine intake.
- Look for ways to share responsibilities with your friends, coworkers and family. Think of specific things people can do to help you reduce your stress.
- Take time each week to discuss issues, plans, schedules and responsibilities with your family, friends and coworkers. Make this a time for teamwork and positive problem solving.
- Get away from work and take time for yourself and loved ones.

ARE YOU GETTING ENOUGH *Z-Z-Z-Z-Z*S?

If you fall asleep within five minutes of lying down, you are likely sleep deprived. How can you change your routine to make sure you get at least seven hours of sleep a night?

Note

1. N. P. Pronk, B. Martinson, R. C. Kessler, et al, "The Association Between Work Performance and Physical Activity, Cardiorespiratory Fitness and Obesity," *Journal of Occupational and Environmental Medicine*, January 2004, 46(1):19-25.

healthy strategies for
social situations!

Special occasions are wonderful times for fellowship and enjoying good food. Unfortunately, much of the focus is on too much of foods that are too high in calories, fat and sugar. Are there certain situations that cause you to give up or give in? It's not uncommon for the holidays or a special get-together to derail your healthy eating plan. Does this mean you can't have any fun at the party? Of course not! What it means is that you need to *anticipate the challenges* and *make a plan* to stick with your healthy goals. Planning ahead is the key to success!

The next time you are attending a party or special get-together, remember some basic rules for success. Before going to the party, picture in your mind how the event will go. What kinds of foods will be there? Anticipate situations and food temptations that will be difficult for you. Imagine yourself in control of your eating and make healthy choices. Set some ground rules for yourself before you get there.

- Fill your plate only one time.
- Limit yourself to small servings.
- Eat something healthful before you go, and enjoy the fellowship instead—never go to a special event hungry.

- Make up your mind to avoid the tempting high-fat, high-calorie choices.
- Ask someone to hold you accountable.
- Decide in advance that you'll only eat a few bites of your favorite food.
- Check out all the available foods before you begin filling your plate, choose only one or two that are your *absolute* favorites and leave the rest behind.
- If it is a potluck event, bring a delicious low-fat version of a favorite. It just might be the hit of the party!
- Eat slowly; it takes about 20 minutes for your brain to get the message that your stomach is full.

KEEP BURNING THE CALORIES

On the day of a special occasion (or for a day or two after), make sure you fit in your physical activity. Taking a brisk walk prior to the event can help curb your appetite. Participating in exercise helps boost motivation and provides encouragement for managing tempting situations. By making an effort to exercise, you may be less likely to load up on chips—you worked too hard to burn those calories! You may have to exercise in the morning or at other times to guarantee you'll fit it in. Be creative and set aside time for physical activity however you can.

FOCUS ON FUN AND FELLOWSHIP

The relationships you build and the fun times will be much more valuable to you than any of the foods you might eat. Decide ahead of time that you'll have a meaningful conversation with several people at the

HAVE A PLAN

You don't have to skip a fun social event! The secret to healthy eating for special occasions is to remember the principles of *balance, moderation* and *variety.*

gathering. Focus on others, rather than on yourself and your appetite. In fact, nutrition and health might be a good topic of conversation. Find a place to talk away from the food line, and try not to eat while talking with other people—hold a low-calorie beverage in your hand instead.

SUCCESS TIPS FOR SPECIFIC OCCASIONS

Business and Meetings

If you're in the business world, you may attend seminars, meetings and other special events. You may also have to travel. If you're not involved in business meetings, you probably attend a lot of meetings anyway: church meetings, Bible study, community meetings, and get-togethers with family and friends. Unfortunately, most of these occasions involve food. By planning ahead you can stick with your goals for a healthy lifestyle.

- **Decide ahead of time to pack your own snacks:** raw vegetables, fruit, low-fat crackers, pretzels or a whole-grain bagel. Bringing your own snack will provide you with a backup in case no healthy foods are offered. It's also a great way to curb your appetite if a meeting runs long.

- **Drink plenty of water.** Avoid high-calorie beverages, such as soft drinks and coffee with cream.

- **Make time for physical activity.** Sitting for hours at a time can cause boredom, which triggers snacking. Even a 5- or 10-minute walk is helpful.

- **Watch out for buffet-style food service.** Load up on fresh fruits, vegetables and other low-fat choices. Don't load your plate just because it's "all you can eat." Rather than trying all the foods, pick one or two of your favorites and keep your portions small.

- **If you're providing the food or bringing a dish, make sure that it's healthy.** Don't feel that you have to please people with high-fat desserts and other foods. You'll be surprised at how appreciative people will be at your thoughtfulness.

Holidays and Parties

Special occasions are celebrated with special foods! During these times, tempting foods are usually everywhere, and everyone is eating them and offering them to you. Know what situations are most difficult for you. With some simple strategies, holidays and parties can be enjoyed without the guilt of overdoing it. Here are some strategies to help get you started.

- Make a commitment to stick with your goals.
- Stick to your regular eating schedule. This will help you avoid the all-day grazing that can sometimes occur when food is always around.
- Eat slowly and concentrate on enjoying the foods you eat.
- Because special foods are a part of the season, taste small portions of the items that are truly unique to the holiday and leave the everyday foods alone.
- Rather than overdoing it every day during the holiday season, plan for one or two special meals you'll really enjoy; make up for these by eating healthy the rest of the time.
- Learn to say "No, thank you." It's okay to turn down food politely. Have a plan for what you'll say. Keep it simple.
- Make sure you take time to relax before and during special occasions and during holidays. Spend some time praying and meditating about ways that will help you stick with your goals.
- Don't allow yourself to gain weight over the holidays; weigh yourself at least once a week. Cut back and resume your eating plan if you notice your weight creeping upward.
- Plan enjoyable activities that are not centered around food; be creative.
- If you're the host, plan to serve healthy foods. Learn to make low-fat substitutions in the recipes for your favorite holiday foods.
- Avoid all-or-nothing thinking; don't deprive yourself or feel guilty about enjoying certain foods.

keeping the
goal in mind!

But one thing I do: Forgetting what is behind and straining
toward what is ahead, I press on toward the goal to win the prize
for which God has called me heavenward in Christ Jesus.

PHILIPPIANS 3:13-14

ere's the most important question to ask when setting a goal: *Is my goal in line with God's desire for my life?* Consider your goal worthwhile and consistent with God's plan for your life if you can answer yes to one or more of the following questions:

- Will achieving my goal help me grow closer to God and serve Him better?
- Will achieving my goal help me feel better about myself and live more effectively?
- Will achieving my goal improve my ability to serve others?
- Will achieving my goal improve my health and well-being?

Prayerfully seek God's wisdom and guidance before moving ahead with your goals and plans. You should also seek wise counsel from trusted family and friends. Remember, it's better to spend several weeks prayerfully considering and developing your goals and plans than it is to start tomorrow toward a goal that you can't (or shouldn't) achieve.

SETTING REALISTIC GOALS

How many times have you made up your mind that you were going to make a change and then fallen short of your goal? Do any of these sound familiar?

- I'll never eat dessert again.
- I'm going to exercise at 7:00 A.M. every day.
- I'm going to spend one hour daily in quiet time.
- I will lose 60 pounds in three months.

It's best to avoid setting too rigid or all-or-none goals that use words such as "never again," "always," "every day" or "must." Setting goals that are unrealistic or too demanding will set you up for failure and disappointment.

Another reason people often fall short of their goals is that they try to take on too much too soon. Realistic goals and a well-thought-out plan are the most important ingredients for success.

DEVELOPING A PLAN

The key to setting goals and building a successful plan is to ask yourself the right questions.

What Do I Want to Accomplish?

Do you really want to achieve a certain weight, or is the underlying issue that you want to feel better about yourself? When setting a goal, it's important to have a clear idea of the benefits you are looking for. Ask yourself how your life will be different when you achieve your goal. How will you feel if you don't achieve it?

What Are My Motivations?

People who are successful in achieving and maintaining long-term goals have clear reasons for doing so. In other words, the reward has to be worth the effort. When setting goals, it's much more important to focus on things you can do rather than on things you wish you could be. Motivations such as improving your relationships, feeling better and improving your health are much stronger motivations than looking better or achieving an ideal body weight for a special event such as a high school reunion or a wedding.

What Steps Do I Need to Take?

When setting goals it's important to have the long-term results in mind, but it's even more important to focus on what you can do each day to achieve them. With each success, you'll gain the confidence and encouragement you need to take the next step.

What Might Keep Me from Reaching My Goal?

Understanding your past successes or failures is a great place to start when setting new goals. Think about some goals you've set for yourself in the past. What worked for you and what didn't? Are you committed to achieving your goal? Are you willing to stick with your plans when times get tough or you experience a setback? Make sure your goals and plans are flexible. You will encounter life changes along the way; be prepared to adjust your expectations.

Who Can Help, and How Can They Help?

It's very difficult to make lifestyle changes without the support of family and friends. Having a solid system of support greatly increases your chances for success. Try to seek out people who have accomplished what you are trying to achieve. Finding family and friends who have goals similar to yours can also be helpful. This step requires some effort on your part; you will have to ask for the

I THINK I CAN . . .

Do you believe it's possible to achieve your goals? If not, you won't be motivated to try. Some goals require diligence and hard work—but persistence pays off. Believe in yourself, and don't let naysayers prove you wrong.

help you need. Don't expect people to understand your needs and volunteer their help.

How Can I Monitor My Progress?

Self-monitoring is one of the best predictors of success when striving for a goal. The ability to see your progress along the way helps keep you motivated and on track. The path to most goals is usually not a straight line. By monitoring your progress, you'll see that a slip-up or two along the way can't reverse all the progress you've made. When setting goals, make sure you build in a plan for monitoring your progress. Have a plan for rewarding yourself as you achieve important victories along the way. Remember, if you don't know what you're aiming for, you'll hit it every time.

your learning
style

*I praise you because I am fearfully and
wonderfully made; your works are wonderful,
I know that full well.*

PSALM 139:14

Scripture tells us that God created us as unique and special, and we can thank Him and praise Him for that truth. But we tend to forget that our uniqueness is not limited to physical appearance, fingerprints and DNA. We receive, process and communicate information in our own unique and special styles, according to the gifts, talents and abilities that God has fashioned into our being.

Expanding on the work of Howard Gardener, educators have discovered that there are eight distinct ways that people process and express information.[1] These are often referred to as "intelligence styles" or "learning styles," but they apply to all aspects of life—including how people relate to God. Read on to discover your unique learning style—a style that reflects a facet of God's own image—and take the opportunity to express your thankfulness in that way.

On the pages that follow, you will find brief descriptions of the eight learning styles. As you read these descriptions, take note of which ones resonate in you and then experiment with the different suggestions listed for each style. You will probably find two or three that fit you most and two or three that fit you least; the remaining styles will fall somewhere in the middle. Use the space in between for notes and thoughts. Once you discover the styles that fit you best, incorporate them into your lifestyle and use them to enhance your time with the Lord.

VERBAL-LINGUISTIC

I will extol the Lord at all times.
His praise will always be on my lips.

PSALM 34:1

Strengths
- Has a natural ability to use words and language
- Understands root meanings of words
- Presents material convincingly
- Makes a good speaker, writer, storyteller and teacher
- Expresses thoughts and emotions most naturally in words

Ways to Use Strengths
- Write in a journal
- Write poems and prayers expressing thankfulness
- Tell stories that illustrate God's faithful love and foster thankfulness in others
- Use humor and wit to captivate listeners
- Give public testimony to God's goodness
- Tell others about First Place 4 Health through written or verbal communication

VISUAL-SPATIAL

He makes me lie down in green pastures,
he leads me beside quiet waters.

PSALM 23:1

Strengths

- Is able to create vivid mental images and then use color, texture and design to portray those images
- Excels at crafts and interior design
- Likes graphs and charts
- Expresses thoughts and emotions in images, colors and designs

Ways to Use Strengths

- Use brightly colored pages in your journal
- Visualize God's goodness and love and express it through art and design
- "Mind map" rather than journal write[2]
- Use stickers, fabric and pictures to express thankfulness
- Create special cards to share with others that give thanks to God through artistic expression

LOGICAL-MATHEMATICAL

"To whom will you compare me?
Or who is my equal?" says the Holy One.

ISAIAH 40:25

Strengths

- Understands logic and numbers
- Has the ability to reason through and connect pieces of information

- Is able to ask questions and reason through complex problems
- Expresses thoughts and emotions in concepts and sequences

Ways to Use Strengths
- Create logical progression sequences that prove God's faithfulness
- Number your journal entries
- Recall chronology of events that lead to thankfulness
- Use God's Word to solve complex problems
- Question and then affirm God's love
- Use reason to convince others of God's faithfulness and love

BODY-KINESTHETIC

For in him we live and move and have our being.

ACTS 17:28

Strengths
- Able to express thought and emotion through movement
- Possesses balance and eye-hand coordination
- Has keen body awareness
- Appreciates the gift of movement
- Expresses thoughts and emotions while in motion

Ways to Use Strengths
- Interpret Scripture through mime or dance
- Praise God while walking or exercising
- Feel God's pleasure while moving your body
- Dance and use hand motions and body language that express gratitude

- Lead your First Place 4 Health group in a charades exercise that expresses God's enduring love and mighty power
- Use your body as a living expression of God's grace

MUSICAL-RHYTHMIC

Let us come before him with thanksgiving
and extol him with music and song.

PSALM 95:2

Strengths

- Produces and appreciates music
- Enjoys praising God through song
- Understands rhythm and tonal patterns
- Can hear sounds others miss
- Can lead others in worship through music
- Expresses thoughts and emotions through sounds, rhythms and patterns

Ways to Use Strengths

- Sing and whistle as you go about your day
- Compose praise songs
- Lead worship through music
- Move in rhythmic patterns
- Recite psalms using the rhythm built into these prayers
- Play musical instruments that give sounds of praise
- Share your gift of music with your First Place 4 Health group so that they can worship through music, too

NATURALIST-ENVIRONMENTAL

Holy, holy, holy is the LORD Almighty;
the whole earth is full of his glory.

ISAIAH 6:3

Strengths

- Has a profound love for animals, plants and nature
- Enjoys communion with the natural world
- Appreciates God's work of creation
- Interested in ecology and conservation
- Expresses thoughts and emotions in terms of nature and creation

Ways to Use Strengths

- Take nature walks and hikes through God's creation
- Connect naturally occurring objects with God's attributes
- Thank God by caring for His world
- Teach others about God's creation
- Take your First Place 4 Health group on a scavenger hunt and help them see God's wonders in nature
- Stop and smell the roses, and teach others to do the same

INTERPERSONAL

How good and pleasant it is when brothers live together in unity!

PSALM 133:1

Strengths

- Has the ability to relate to and understand others
- Maintains peace in group settings

- Encourages others to join in fellowship
- Great organizational skills
- Expresses thoughts and emotions in group settings

Ways to Use Strengths

- Create a small group to pray and discuss personal areas of struggle
- Share blessings with others through phone calls and personal visits
- Join or start a prayer-chain ministry in your church and First Place 4 Health group
- Help with celebration gatherings
- Encourage others to join you in thankfulness
- Share your love of people with everyone you meet

INTRAPERSONAL

Find rest, O my soul, in God alone; my hope comes from him.

PSALM 62:5

Strengths

- Self-reflective and aware
- Understands dreams, visions and process
- Enjoys silence and solitude
- Is able to grasp and think through spiritual truth
- Expresses thoughts and emotions through introspection

Ways to Use Strengths

- Meditate on God and His goodness
- Reason within yourself to overcome doubts and fears
- Find discernment in stillness and silence

- Be still and allow God's goodness to resonate in your soul
- Practice contemplative prayer and teach others to do the same
- Share your gift of meditation with your First Place 4 Health group

Which three learning styles best fit you?

How can you combine these strengths to create a style of learning and expression that is uniquely your own?

What can you do today to begin incorporating your unique style of learning into your daily life?

Notes

1. Adapted from Howard Gardner, *Intelligence Reframed: Multiple Intelligences for the 21st Century* (New York: Basic Books, 2000).
2. A "mind map" is a form of outlining or categorizing your thoughts. In mind mapping, a central thought is put in the center of the "map" and the thoughts are written around it in a road-map fashion. For a complete explanation, go to http://en.wikipedia.org/wiki/Mind_map.

creating a
thankfulness journal

O Lord my God, I will give you thanks forever.

PSALM 30:12

One of the easiest ways to foster an attitude of thankfulness is to create a thankfulness journal: a separate place to record the simple everyday things for which you are grateful. Even though you already make daily entries in a prayer journal or spiritual diary, keeping a thankfulness journal is an essential exercise to develop a heart that gives thanks in all circumstances. Unlike other forms of journal writing, a thankfulness journal is for the specific purpose of recording the things for which you are thankful. It serves as both an acknowledgment of what God has done for you and as a daily challenge to look for things to be thankful for, even on bad days. Keeping a thankfulness journal is the ongoing practice of recording God's ongoing grace.

Perhaps keeping a written list of "What I am thankful for today" seems too simplistic to be effective, yet studies have proven the positive impact of maintaining a thankfulness journal. Researchers have discovered that those who keep thankfulness journals on a daily basis exercise more regularly, have fewer health problems, make greater progress toward important personal goals, experience less depression, handle stress more effectively and have more energy and vitality. They even sleep better at night![1] Spiritual teachers throughout the ages have maintained that those with thankful hearts reap God's choicest blessings. Isn't it amazing that something as simple as keeping a thankfulness journal can change the quality of life so drastically?

Another plus is that keeping a thankfulness journal is not only beneficial, but it is also fun. Here are some basic steps to help you get started.

Start It Now

Any kind of notebook will do for a thankfulness journal. The important thing is that your gratitude pages are bound together and kept in a safe place rather than randomly scribbled on loose pieces of paper scattered here and there. Some folks like to decorate the cover of their thankfulness journal; others like to draw pictures that describe the things and events for which they are thankful. A stationery store, an arts and crafts retailer or scrapbook supply store will have ideas for customizing your journal. The more unique and personal the pages, the more likely you are to visit the journal consistently. Most people find that they want enough space in their journal to record two to three month's worth of gratitude affirmations.

Create your thankfulness journal and then complete the remainder of this section. Each section will give you an opportunity to begin filling your new "thankfulness bank."

Keep It Simple

Unlike other spiritual journals, a thankfulness journal is not a place to process your feelings, cry out in lament or pour out your heart to God. The whole purpose of a thankfulness journal is to thank God for blessing you in ways too numerous to adequately recount. The pages will consist largely of one- to two-sentence statements beginning with "I am thankful for . . ." You can add drawings, mementos or small photographs to enrich your simple words. Try using colored pencils to add color and texture, or experiment with stickers or glitter. Your creativity is a precious gift from God that you are called to use in expressing your thankfulness to Him.

Place a Scripture heading at the top of each day's page to remind you exactly Who you are thanking. Searching the Scriptures for thankfulness verses each day and committing some of those verses to memory will play a key role in developing a lifestyle of thankfulness.

As your first entry in your thankfulness journal, write a short statement expressing your thankfulness to God for a simple, everyday pleasure. Now draw a small picture next to your sentence that creatively expresses your gratitude.

Keep It Private

This is your journal, with your personal thoughts recorded for your benefit and God's glory. If you write thinking that others might read your words, you will tend to write what you want them to hear! You can share your thoughts with trusted others, but the pages of this sacred journal are intended for your eyes only. God, who sees what you write on these private pages, will reward you (see Matthew 6:6).

Share a private thanksgiving with God in your thankfulness journal.

Keep It Honest

Only you and God are going to see what is written on these pages, so there is absolutely no reason to exaggerate, minimize or force your feelings. List only those things for which you are genuinely grateful. God knows your thoughts before you even write them on the page (see Psalm 139:4). This is not a place for pious platitudes or lofty idealism. Heartfelt gratitude is always about the truth as it applies to your life in the present moment.

Write a thankfulness truth that applies to your life in the present moment.

Keep It Personal

Comparisons and judgments have no place in your thankfulness journal. This journal is about you and your relationship with God, not about your neighbors. Remember, the Pharisee whom Jesus criticized prayed, "God, I thank you that I am not like all other men" (Luke 18:11). We never need to fill our cup of thankfulness by devaluing another human being or feeding our ego at another's expense. Gratitude is about giving thanks to God for the wonderful things He has done for us, not telling Him what wonderful things we have done for Him.

List one great thing God has done for you that fills you with joy.

Keep It Specific

Rather than writing generalized statements such as, "I am thankful that God is faithful," write about a specific instance that reminded you of God's faithfulness. Perhaps you saw or heard something today that brought God's loving-kindness to memory. For example, rather than being thankful for the sun, write about how the sun touched your skin and brought warmth to your soul.

What recent occurrence reminded you of God's loving-kindness? Write it down as a thank offering in your journal.

Keep It God-Affirming

We should only be grateful for sources of health and healing, never for anything that erodes our relationship with God, damages His creation or harms our neighbor. Likewise, we can never be truly thankful for anything that offends God's Holy Spirit who resides in our heart, or that destroys our body, His earthly temple (see 1 Corinthians 6:19-20). With this in mind, you can use your thankfulness journal as a type of accountability partner. Ask yourself, "Is this something I can write about in my thankfulness journal?" If the answer is no, then it is not a beneficial endeavor.

Think of something you have done today that you cannot write about with thankfulness. Now thank God that He forgives you for doing that specific thing.

Keep It Consistent

Make adding entries to your thankfulness journal a daily habit. Begin by writing down five simple pleasures for which you are thankful each morning when you first wake up. Before you go to bed that night, record another five things for which you are thankful. Five each morning, five each evening—seven days a week.

Perhaps you are thinking, *I couldn't possibly find 70 things to be thankful for each week!* Remember, we are *training* our minds to develop a lifestyle of thankfulness. We must fight the scarcity mentality that makes us fear that we will not have enough thankfulness to write 70 "I am thankful" sentences each week. Just write down five in the morning and five in the evening today and trust that there will be five in the morning and five in the evening tomorrow.

Although writing prayers in your thankfulness journal should not be normal practice, compose a prayer that expresses your commitment to keep your journal daily. Remember, when we commit our plans to the Lord, they will succeed (see Proverbs 16:3).

Review It Often

Reread your thankfulness entries often, especially on days when you need to be reminded of God's faithful love. Once a month, carve out time to read all 280-plus entries that you made during the month and bask in the warmth of God's love and care. As you notice a gradual shift in your outlook and attitude, be sure to thank God for that too. Each time you thank God, He will give you even more reasons to thank Him! You will be amazed at how God will bring health and healing as you faithfully practice giving Him thanks in all circumstances. God delights in those who delight in Him, and He showers them with His abundant blessings.

"You are my God, and I will give you thanks." PSALM 118:28

Date: _____

You are my God. This morning I give you thanks for:

1. _____
_____

2. _____
_____

3. _____
_____

4. _____
_____

5. _____
_____

Tonight I am especially thankful for:

1. _____
_____

2. _____
_____

3. _____
_____

4. _____
_____

5. _____
_____

Note

1. Robert A. Emmons and Michael E. McCullough, "Highlights from the Research Project on Gratitude and Thankfulness." http://www.psy.miami.edu/faculty/mmccullough/grati tude/highlights_fall_2003.pdf (accessed April 2005).

your personality
profile

There has been much discussion about whether we are born with our personality or whether our environment shapes who we are. Many studies of twins separated at birth and raised apart indicate that each of us is born with our own distinct personality. Many times the way we think about people affects the way we treat them. Understanding and appreciating that God has given each person his or her personality can help us understand and react appropriately when we bump up against thinking that is different from our way of thinking.

In the workplace, knowing coworkers' personality types can help us work more productively and peacefully with others. In the home, knowing the personality types of our children can help us to train them according to their personality tendencies. Proverbs 22:6 tells us to "train a child in the way he should go, and when he is old he will not turn from it."

There are many personality inventories available today. You have probably heard of the Myers-Briggs Type Indicator, the most common inventory used in the workplace. DISC is another used in many churches. Gary Smalley and John Trent have used animals to describe the four different personality types, while Tim LaHaye has used Bible characters.

Florence Littauer has authored more than 15 books about personalities. In her books, she uses terms coined by Hippocrates more than

2,000 years ago. With Florence's permission, we have chosen to use the easy-to-understand and easy-to-teach information from her book *Your Personality Tree* to help you discover your personality type.[1]

Florence describes four personality types: sanguine, choleric, melancholic and phlegmatic. Most of us are a blend of two personality types, and it is important to know our personality type blend as we interact with other people and seek to become the person God intends us to be. Knowing the characteristics that are common to our personality type can also help us understand what challenges lie ahead as we ask God to change our thought patterns:

> We demolish arguments and every pretension that sets itself up against the knowledge of God, and we take captive every thought to make it obedient to Christ (2 Corinthians 10:5).

Here is a brief explanation of each personality type, and how they approach First Place 4 Health:

- **Sanguines** need the First Place 4 Health program to be fun, and they lose interest when the program isn't entertaining. They thrive on receiving attention when they do well.

- **Cholerics** like to control the way they do the First Place 4 Health program. The popular Nike phrase *Just Do It!* is a perfect slogan for this personality type.

- **Melancholics** want to do First Place 4 Health perfectly and tend to become discouraged when perfection isn't possible.

- **Phlegmatics** want a program to be easy. Giving them bite-sized elements of First Place 4 Health can help get them started and stay focused.

Knowing our personality type can help us understand why we approach the First Place 4 Health program from different vantage points.

PERSONALITY PROFILE[2]

Place a check in the box next to the one word in each line that most often describes you. Be sure to complete all 40 lines. If you are not sure which word applies, ask your spouse or a friend, or think about what your answer would have been when you were a child. (See the Personality Test Word Definitions beginning on page 88 for the most accurate results.)

Strengths

1.	❐ Adventurous	❐ Adaptable	❐ Animated	❐ Analytical
2.	❐ Persistent	❐ Playful	❐ Persuasive	❐ Peaceful
3.	❐ Submissive	❐ Self-sacrificing	❐ Sociable	❐ Strong-willed
4.	❐ Considerate	❐ Controlled	❐ Competitive	❐ Convincing
5.	❐ Refreshing	❐ Respectful	❐ Reserved	❐ Resourceful
6.	❐ Satisfied	❐ Sensitive	❐ Self-reliant	❐ Spirited
7.	❐ Planner	❐ Patient	❐ Positive	❐ Promoter
8.	❐ Sure	❐ Spontaneous	❐ Scheduled	❐ Shy
9.	❐ Orderly	❐ Obliging	❐ Outspoken	❐ Optimistic
10.	❐ Friendly	❐ Faithful	❐ Funny	❐ Forceful
11.	❐ Daring	❐ Delightful	❐ Diplomatic	❐ Detailed
12.	❐ Cheerful	❐ Consistent	❐ Cultured	❐ Confident
13.	❐ Idealistic	❐ Independent	❐ Inoffensive	❐ Inspiring
14.	❐ Demonstrative	❐ Decisive	❐ Dry humor	❐ Deep
15.	❐ Mediator	❐ Musical	❐ Mover	❐ Mixes easily
16.	❐ Thoughtful	❐ Tenacious	❐ Talker	❐ Tolerant
17.	❐ Listener	❐ Loyal	❐ Leader	❐ Lively
18.	❐ Contented	❐ Chief	❐ Chart maker	❐ Cute
19.	❐ Perfectionist	❐ Pleasant	❐ Productive	❐ Popular
20.	❐ Bouncy	❐ Bold	❐ Behaved	❐ Balanced

Weaknesses

21.	❐ Blank	❐ Bashful	❐ Brassy	❐ Bossy
22.	❐ Undisciplined	❐ Unsympathetic	❐ Unenthusiastic	❐ Unforgiving
23.	❐ Reticent	❐ Resentful	❐ Resistant	❐ Repetitious
24.	❐ Fussy	❐ Fearful	❐ Forgetful	❐ Frank

25.	❏ Impatient	❏ Insecure	❏ Indecisive	❏ Interrupts
26.	❏ Unpopular	❏ Uninvolved	❏ Unpredictable	❏ Unaffectionate
27.	❏ Headstrong	❏ Haphazard	❏ Hard to please	❏ Hesitant
28.	❏ Plain	❏ Pessimistic	❏ Proud	❏ Permissive
29.	❏ Angered easily	❏ Aimless	❏ Argumentative	❏ Alienated
30.	❏ Naive	❏ Negative attitude	❏ Nervy	❏ Nonchalant
31.	❏ Worrier	❏ Withdrawn	❏ Workaholic	❏ Wants credit
32.	❏ Too sensitive	❏ Tactless	❏ Timid	❏ Talkative
33.	❏ Doubtful	❏ Disorganized	❏ Domineering	❏ Depressed
34.	❏ Inconsistent	❏ Introvert	❏ Intolerant	❏ Indifferent
35.	❏ Messy	❏ Moody	❏ Mumbles	❏ Manipulative
36.	❏ Slow	❏ Stubborn	❏ Show-off	❏ Skeptical
37.	❏ Loner	❏ Lord over others	❏ Lazy	❏ Loud
38.	❏ Sluggish	❏ Suspicious	❏ Short-tempered	❏ Scatterbrained
39.	❏ Revengeful	❏ Restless	❏ Reluctant	❏ Rash
40.	❏ Compromising	❏ Critical	❏ Crafty	❏ Changeable

PERSONALITY SCORING SHEET

Transfer all your check marks from your profile to the corresponding words on this score sheet. For example, if you checked "animated" in line 1, also check it on the scoring sheet's line 1. (**Note:** Although the same four words for each line are used on the scoring sheet as were used on the profile, they are arranged in a different order on the scoring sheet. Carefully transfer your check marks to make sure you don't check the wrong word!)

Strengths

	Popular Sanguine	*Powerful Choleric*	*Perfect Melancholic*	*Peaceful Phlegmatic*
1.	❏ Animated	❏ Adventurous	❏ Analytical	❏ Adaptable
2.	❏ Playful	❏ Persuasive	❏ Persistent	❏ Peaceful
3.	❏ Sociable	❏ Strong-willed	❏ Self-sacrificing	❏ Submissive
4.	❏ Convincing	❏ Competitive	❏ Considerate	❏ Controlled
5.	❏ Refreshing	❏ Resourceful	❏ Respectful	❏ Reserved
6.	❏ Spirited	❏ Self-reliant	❏ Sensitive	❏ Satisfied

7.	❐ Promoter	❐ Positive	❐ Planner	❐ Patient
8.	❐ Spontaneous	❐ Sure	❐ Scheduled	❐ Shy
9.	❐ Optimistic	❐ Outspoken	❐ Orderly	❐ Obliging
10.	❐ Funny	❐ Forceful	❐ Faithful	❐ Friendly
11.	❐ Delightful	❐ Daring	❐ Detailed	❐ Diplomatic
12.	❐ Cheerful	❐ Confident	❐ Cultured	❐ Consistent
13.	❐ Inspiring	❐ Independent	❐ Idealistic	❐ Inoffensive
14.	❐ Demonstrative	❐ Decisive	❐ Deep	❐ Dry humor
15.	❐ Mixes easily	❐ Mover	❐ Musical	❐ Mediator
16.	❐ Talker	❐ Tenacious	❐ Thoughtful	❐ Tolerant
17.	❐ Lively	❐ Leader	❐ Loyal	❐ Listener
18.	❐ Cute	❐ Chief	❐ Chart maker	❐ Contented
19.	❐ Popular	❐ Productive	❐ Perfectionist	❐ Pleasant
20.	❐ Bouncy	❐ Bold	❐ Behaved	❐ Balanced
TOTALS:				

Weaknesses

	Popular Sanguine	Powerful Choleric	Perfect Melancholic	Peaceful Phlegmatic
21.	❐ Brassy	❐ Bossy	❐ Bashful	❐ Blank
22.	❐ Undisciplined	❐ Unsympathetic	❐ Unforgiving	❐ Unenthusiastic
23.	❐ Repetitious	❐ Resistant	❐ Resentful	❐ Reticent
24.	❐ Forgetful	❐ Frank	❐ Fussy	❐ Fearful
25.	❐ Interrupts	❐ Impatient	❐ Insecure	❐ Indecisive
26.	❐ Unpredictable	❐ Unaffectionate	❐ Unpopular	❐ Uninvolved
27.	❐ Haphazard	❐ Headstrong	❐ Hard to please	❐ Hesitant
28.	❐ Permissive	❐ Proud	❐ Pessimistic	❐ Plain
29.	❐ Angered easily	❐ Argumentative	❐ Alienated	❐ Aimless
30.	❐ Naive	❐ Nervy	❐ Negative attitude	❐ Nonchalant
31.	❐ Wants credit	❐ Workaholic	❐ Withdrawn	❐ Worrier
32.	❐ Talkative	❐ Tactless	❐ Too sensitive	❐ Timid
33.	❐ Disorganized	❐ Domineering	❐ Depressed	❐ Doubtful
34.	❐ Inconsistent	❐ Intolerant	❐ Introvert	❐ Indifferent
35.	❐ Messy	❐ Manipulative	❐ Moody	❐ Mumbles
36.	❐ Show-off	❐ Stubborn	❐ Skeptical	❐ Slow
37.	❐ Loud	❐ Lord over others	❐ Loner	❐ Lazy

38.	⊐ Scatterbrained	⊐ Short-tempered	⊐ Suspicious	⊐ Sluggish
39.	⊐ Restless	⊐ Rash	⊐ Revengeful	⊐ Reluctant
40.	⊐ Changeable	⊐ Crafty	⊐ Critical	⊐ Compromising
TOTALS:				
Combined Totals:				

After you have transferred your answers, add up the total number of check marks in each of the four columns, and then add your totals from both the Strengths and Weaknesses sections. Your combined score will indicate your dominant personality type and also your personality combination. For example, if you score 35 in both the Powerful Choleric strengths and the Powerful Choleric weaknesses, there's little question as to your personality type: You're almost all Powerful Choleric. If, however, you score 16 in Powerful Choleric, 14 in Perfect Melancholic and 5 in each of the others, your personality type is a Powerful Choleric with a strong Perfect Melancholic. Of course, you will also learn your least-dominant personality characteristic.

Once you have identified your personality type, you can then begin to learn how to put your strengths to work for you in the First Place 4 Health program and how to compensate for your weaknesses. You can also use what you learn about the different personality types to encourage others in your First Place 4 Health group in ways that are most beneficial to their personality type!

PERSONALITY TEST WORD DEFINITIONS

Strengths

1

Adventurous. Will take on new and daring enterprises with a determination to master them.

Adaptable. Easily fits and is comfortable in any situation.

Animated. Full of life; lively use of hand, arm and face gestures.

Analytical. Likes to examine the parts for their logical and proper relationships.

2

Persistent. Sees one project through to its completion before starting another.

Playful. Full of fun and good humor.

Persuasive. Convinces through logic and fact rather than charm or power.

Peaceful. Seems undisturbed and tranquil and retreats from any form of strife.

3

Submissive. Easily accepts any other's point of view or desire with little need to assert his or her own opinion.

Self-sacrificing. Willingly gives up his or her own personal being for the sake of or to meet the needs of others.

Sociable. Sees being with others as an opportunity to be cute and entertaining rather than as a challenge or business opportunity.

Strong-willed. Determined to have one's own way.

4

Considerate. Having regard for the needs and feelings of others.

Controlled. Has emotional feelings but rarely displays them.

Competitive. Turns every situation, happening, or game into a contest and always plays to win!

Convincing. Can win others over to anything through the sheer charm of his or her personality.

5

Refreshing. Renews and stimulates or makes others feel good.

Respectful. Treats others with deference, honor and esteem.

Reserved. Self-restrained in expression of emotion or enthusiasm.

Resourceful. Able to act quickly and effectively in virtually all situations.

6

Satisfied. Easily accepts any circumstance or situation.

Sensitive. Intensively cares about others and what happens.

Self-reliant. Independent and can fully rely on his or her own capabilities, judgment and resources.

Spirited. Full of life and excitement.

7

Planner. Prefers to work out a detailed arrangement beforehand for the accomplishment of a project or goal and prefers involvement with the planning stages and the finished product rather than the carrying out of the task.

Patient. Unmoved by delay, remains calm and tolerant.

Positive. Knows it will turn out right if he or she is in charge.

Promoter. Urges or compels others to go along, join or invest through the charm of his or her own personality.

8

Sure. Confident, rarely hesitates or wavers.

Spontaneous. Prefers all of life to be impulsive, unpremeditated activity, not restricted by plans.

Scheduled. Makes, and lives, according to a daily plan; dislikes his or her plan to be interrupted.

Shy. Quiet, doesn't easily instigate a conversation.

9

Orderly. Having a methodical, systematic arrangement of things.

Obliging. Accommodating; is quick to do it another's way.

Outspoken. Speaks frankly and without reserve.

Optimistic. Sunny disposition who convinces self and others that everything will turn out all right.

10

Friendly. A responder rather than an initiator; seldom starts a conversation.

Faithful. Consistently reliable, steadfast, loyal and devoted, sometimes beyond reason.

Funny. Sparkling sense of humor that can make virtually any story into a hilarious event.

Forceful. A commanding personality whom others would hesitate to take a stand against.

11

Daring. Willing to take risks, fearless, bold.

Delightful. Is upbeat and fun to be with.

Diplomatic. Deals with people tactfully, sensitively and patiently.

Detailed. Does everything in proper order with a clear memory of all the things that happen.

12

Cheerful. Consistently in good spirits and promoting happiness in others.

Consistent. Tends to stay emotionally on an even keel, responding as one might expect.

Cultured. Interests involve both intellectual and artistic pursuits, such as theatre, symphony, ballet.

Confident. Self-assured and certain of own ability and success.

13

Idealistic. Visualizes things in their perfect form and has a need to measure up to that standard himself or herself.

Independent. Self-sufficient, self-supporting, self-confident and seems to have little need of help.

Inoffensive. Never says or causes anything unpleasant or objectionable.

Inspiring. Encourages others to work, join or be involved, and makes the whole thing fun.

14

Demonstrative. Openly expresses emotion, especially affection, and doesn't hesitate to touch others while speaking to them.

Decisive. Has quick, conclusive, judgment-making ability.

Dry humor. Exhibits "dry wit," usually one-liners that can be sarcastic in nature.

Deep. Intense and often introspective with a distaste for surface conversation and pursuits.

15

Mediator. Consistently finds himself or herself in the role of reconciling differences in order to avoid conflict.

Musical. Participates in or has a deep appreciation for music; is committed to music as an art form, rather than the fun of performance.

Mover. Driven by a need to be productive; is a leader whom others follow; finds it difficult to sit still.

Mixes easily. Loves a party and can't wait to meet everyone in the room; never meets a stranger.

16

Thoughtful. Considerate, remembers special occasions, and is quick to make a kind gesture.

Tenacious. Holds on firmly, stubbornly, and won't let go until the goal is accomplished.

Talker. Constantly talking, generally telling funny stories and entertaining everyone around, feeling the need to fill the silence in order to make others comfortable.

Tolerant. Easily accepts the thoughts and ways of others without the need to disagree with or change them.

17

Listener. Always seems willing to hear what others have to say.

Loyal. Faithful to a person, ideal or job, sometimes beyond reason.

Leader. Is a natural-born director who is driven to be in charge and often finds it difficult to believe that anyone else can do the job as well.

Lively. Full of life, vigorous, energetic.

18

Contented. Easily satisfied with what he or she has, rarely envious.

Chief. Commands leadership and expects people to follow.

Chartmaker. Organizes life, tasks and problem solving by making lists, forms or graphs.

Cute. Precious, adorable, center of attention.

19

Perfectionist. Places high standards on himself or herself, and often on others, desiring that everything be in proper order at all times.

Pleasant. Easygoing, easy to be around, easy to talk with.

Productive. Must constantly be working or achieving, often finds it very difficult to rest.

Popular. Life of the party, and therefore much desired as a party guest.

20

Bouncy. A bubbly, lively personality, full of energy.

Bold. Fearless, daring, forward, unafraid of risk.

Behaved. Consistently desires to conduct himself or herself within the realm of what he or she feels is proper.

Balanced. Stable, middle-of-the-road personality, not subject to sharp highs or lows.

Weaknesses

21

Blank. Shows little facial expression or emotion.

Bashful. Shrinks from getting attention, a result of his or her self-consciousness.

Brassy. Showy, flashy, comes on strong, too loud.

Bossy. Commanding, domineering, sometimes overbearing in adult relationships.

22

Undisciplined. Lack of order permeates most every area of his or her life.

Unsympathetic. Finds it difficult to relate to the problems or hurts of others.

Unenthusiastic. Tends to not get excited, often feeling it won't work anyway.

Unforgiving. Has difficulty forgiving or forgetting a hurt or injustice done to them, likely to hold on to a grudge.

23

Reticent. Unwilling or struggles against getting involved, especially when the situation is complex.

Resentful. Often holds ill feelings as a result of real or imagined offenses.

Resistant. Strives, works against, or hesitates to accept any other way but his or her own.

Repetitious. Retells stories and incidents to entertain without realizing he or she has already told the story several times before, constantly needs to have something to say.

24

Fussy. Insistent over petty matters or details, calling for a great attention to trivial details.

Fearful. Often experiences feelings of deep concern, apprehension or anxiousness.

Forgetful. Lack of memory, which is usually tied to a lack of discipline, and not bothering to mentally record things that aren't fun.

Frank. Straightforward, outspoken and doesn't mind telling others exactly what he or she thinks.

25

Impatient. Finds it difficult to endure irritation or wait for others.

Insecure. Is apprehensive or lacks confidence.

Indecisive. Finds it difficult to make any decision at all (not the personality that labors long over each decision in order to make the perfect one).

Interrupts. Is more of a talker than a listener, starts speaking without even realizing someone else is already speaking.

26

Unpopular. Intensity and demand for perfection can push others away.

Uninvolved. Has no desire to listen or become interested in clubs, groups, activities or other people's lives.

Unpredictable. May be ecstatic one moment and down the next, or willing to help but then disappears, or promises to come but forgets to show up.

Unaffectionate. Finds it difficult to verbally or physically demonstrate tenderness openly.

27

Headstrong. Insists on having his or her own way.

Haphazard. Has no consistent way of doing things.

Hard to please. Has standard set so high that it is difficult to ever satisfy them.

Hesitant. Slow to get moving and hard to get involved.

28

Plain. Has a middle-of-the-road personality without highs or lows and shows little, if any, emotion.

Pessimistic. Hopes for the best but generally sees the downside of a situation first.

Proud. Has great self-esteem and sees himself or herself as always right and the best person for the job.

Permissive. Allows others (including children) to do as they please in order to keep from being disliked.

29

Angered easily. Has a childlike flash-in-the-pan temper that expresses itself in tantrum style, which is over and forgotten almost instantly.

Aimless. Not a goal-setter and has little desire to be one.

Argumentative. Incites arguments because he or she is right, no matter what the situation may be.

Alienated. Easily feels estranged from others, often because of insecurity or fear that others don't really enjoy his or her company.

30

Naive. Simple and childlike perspective, lacking sophistication or comprehension of what the deeper levels of life are really about.

Negative attitude. Attitude is seldom positive; often able to see only the down or dark side of each situation.

Nervy. Full of confidence, fortitude and sheer guts, often in a negative sense.

Nonchalant. Easy-going, unconcerned, indifferent.

31

Worrier. Consistently feels uncertain, troubled or anxious.

Withdrawn. Pulls into himself or herself and needs a great deal of alone or isolation time.

Workaholic. An aggressive goal-setter who must be constantly productive and feels very guilty when resting, is not driven by a need for perfection or completion but by a need for accomplishment and reward.

Wants credit. Thrives on the credit or approval of others. As an entertainer, this person feeds on the applause, laughter and/or acceptance of an audience.

32

Too sensitive. Overly introspective and easily offended when misunderstood.

Tactless. Sometimes expresses himself or herself in a somewhat offensive and inconsiderate way.

Timid. Shrinks from difficult situations.

Talkative. An entertaining, compulsive talker who finds it difficult to listen.

33

Doubtful. Characterized by uncertainty and lack of confidence that it will ever work out.

Disorganized. Lack of ability to ever get life in order.

Domineering. Compulsively takes control of situations and/or people, usually telling others what to do.

Depressed. Feels down much of the time.

34

Inconsistent. Erratic, contradictory, with actions and emotions not based on logic.

Introvert. A person whose thoughts and interest are directed inward, lives within himself or herself.

Intolerant. Appears unable to withstand or accept another's attitudes, point of view or way of doing things.

Indifferent. Feels most things don't matter one way or the other.

35

Messy. Lives in a state of disorder, unable to find things.

Moody. Doesn't get very high emotionally but easily slips into low lows, often when feeling unappreciated.

Mumbles. Will talk quietly under his or her breath when pushed, doesn't bother to speak clearly.

Manipulative. Influences or manages shrewdly or deviously for his or her own advantage, will get his or her way somehow.

36

Slow. Doesn't often act or think quickly, too much of a bother.

Stubborn. Determined to exert his or her own will, not easily persuaded, obstinate.

Show-off. Needs to be the center of attention, wants to be watched.

Skeptical. Disbelieving, questioning the motive behind the words.

37

Loner. Requires a lot of private time and tends to avoid other people.

Lord over. Doesn't hesitate to let others know that he or she is right or is in control.

Lazy. Evaluates work or activity in terms of how much energy it will take.

Loud. Has a laugh or voice that can be heard above others in the room.

38

Sluggish. Slow to get started, needs push to be motivated.

Suspicious. Tends to suspect or distrust others or ideas.

Short-tempered. Has a demanding impatience-based anger and a short fuse. Anger is expressed when others are not moving fast enough or have not completed what they have been asked to do.

Scatterbrained. Lacks the power of concentration or attention, flighty.

39

Revengeful. Knowingly or otherwise holds a grudge and punishes the offender, often by subtly withholding friendship or affection.

Restless. Likes constant new activity because it isn't fun to do the same things all the time.

Reluctant. Unwilling or struggles against getting involved.

Rash. May act hastily without thinking things through—generally because of impatience.

40

Compromising. Will often relax his or her position, even when right, in order to avoid conflict.

Critical. Constantly evaluating and making judgments, frequently thinking or expressing negative reactions.

Crafty. Shrewd, one who can always find a way to get to the desired end.

Changeable. A childlike, short attention span that needs a lot of change and variety to keep from getting bored.

AN OVERVIEW OF THE PERSONALITY TYPES

Popular Sanguines

Motto: "Let's do it the fun way."

Desire: to have fun

Emotional needs: attention, affection, approval, acceptance

Key strengths: ability to talk about anything at any time at any place, bubbling personality, optimism, sense of humor, storytelling ability and enjoyment of people

Key weaknesses: disorganized, can't remember details or names, exaggerates, not serious about anything, trusts others to do the work, too gullible and naive

Get depressed when: life is no fun and no one seems to love them

Are afraid of: being unpopular or bored, having to live by the clock and having to keep a record of money spent

Like people who: listen and laugh, praise and approve

Dislike people who: criticize, don't respond to their humor, or don't think they are cute

Are valuable in the workplace for: their colorful creativity, optimism, light touch, ability to cheer up others and ability to entertain

Could improve if: they became organized, didn't talk so much and learned to tell time

As leaders: they excite, persuade and inspire others; exude charm and entertain; are forgetful and poor on follow-through

Tend to marry: Perfect Melancholics who are sensitive and serious but whom they quickly tire of having to cheer up and by whom they soon tire of being made to feel inadequate or stupid

React to stress by: leaving the scene, going shopping, finding a fun group, creating excuses and blaming others

Recognized by: their constant talking, loud volume and bright eyes

Powerful Cholerics

Motto: "Let's do it my way."

Desire: to have control

Emotional needs: sense of obedience, appreciation for accomplishments and credit for ability

Key strengths: the ability to take charge of anything instantly and to make quick, correct judgments

Key weaknesses: too bossy, domineering, autocratic, insensitive, impatient, unwilling to delegate or give credit to others

Get depressed when: life is out of control and people won't do things their way

Are afraid of: losing control of anything (e.g., losing a job, not being promoted, becoming seriously ill, having a rebellious child or unsupportive mate)

Like people who: are supportive and submissive, see things their way, cooperate quickly and let them take credit

Dislike people who: are lazy and not interested in working constantly, buck their authority, become independent or aren't loyal

Are valuable in the workplace for: their ability to accomplish more than anyone else in a shorter time and because they are usually right

Could improve if: they allowed others to make decisions, delegated authority, became more patient and didn't expect everyone to produce as they do

As leaders: they have a natural feel for being in charge, a quick sense of what will work, a sincere belief in their ability to achieve, and a potential to overwhelm less aggressive people

Tend to marry: Peaceful Phlegmatics who will quietly obey and not buck their authority but who never accomplish enough or get excited over their projects

React to stress by: tightening control, working harder, exercising more or getting rid of the offender

Recognized by: their fast-moving approach, quick grab for control, self-confidence, restless and overpowering attitude

Perfect Melancholics

Motto: "Let's do it the right way."

Desire: to have it right

Emotional needs: a sense of stability, space, silence, sensitivity and support

Key strengths: the ability to organize and set long-range goals, have high standards and ideals and analyze deeply

Key weaknesses: easily depressed, too much time on preparation, too focused on details, remembers negatives and suspicious of others

Get depressed when: life is out of order, standards aren't met, and no one seems to care

Are afraid of: no one understanding how they really feel, making a mistake and having to compromise standards

Like people who: are serious, intellectual, deep and will carry on a sensible conversation

Dislike people who: are lightweights, forgetful, late, disorganized, superficial, prevaricating and unpredictable

Are valuable in the workplace for: their sense of detail, love of analysis, follow-through, high standards of performance and compassion for the hurting

Could improve if: they didn't take life quite so seriously and didn't insist that others be perfectionists

As leaders: they organize well, are sensitive to people's feelings, have deep creativity and want quality performance

Tend to marry: Popular Sanguines for their outgoing personality and social skills, but whom they soon attempt to quiet and get on a schedule

React to stress by: withdrawing, getting lost in a book, becoming depressed, giving up and recounting their problems

Recognized by: their serious and sensitive nature, well-mannered approach, self-deprecating comments, and meticulous and well-groomed looks

Peaceful Phlegmatic

Motto: "Let's do it the easy way."

Desire: to avoid conflict, keep peace

Emotional needs: a sense of respect, feeling of worth, understanding and emotional support

Key strengths: balance, even disposition, dry sense of humor and pleasing personality

Key weaknesses: lack of decisiveness, enthusiasm, energy and a hidden will of iron

Get depressed when: life is full of conflict, they have to face a personal confrontation, no one wants to help and the buck stops with them

Are afraid of: having to deal with a major personal problem, being left holding the bag and making major changes

Like people who: will make decisions for them, will recognize their strengths, will not ignore them and will give them respect

Dislike people who: are too pushy, too loud and expect too much of them

Are valuable in the workplace because: they mediate between contentious people and objectively solve problems

Could improve if: they set goals and became self-motivated, were willing to do more and move faster than expected, and could face their own problems as well as they handle those of others

As leaders: they keep calm, cool and collected; don't make impulsive decisions; are well-liked and inoffensive; and won't cause trouble but don't often come up with brilliant new ideas

Tend to marry: Powerful Cholerics who are strong and decisive, but by whom they soon tire of being pushed around and looked down upon

React to stress by: hiding from it, watching TV, eating and generally tuning out life

Recognized by: their calm approach and relaxed posture (sitting or leaning when possible)

Notes

1. Florence Littauer, *Your Personality Tree* (Dallas, TX: Word Publishing, 1986).
2. Created by Fred Littauer for Florence Littauer, *After Every Wedding Comes a Marriage* (Eugene, OR: Harvest House Publishers, 1981). Used by permission.

Physical Well-Being

dietary supplements—
miracle or myth?

I t seems like every time you turn around, there is new information available about vitamins, minerals and other supplements. If you are like most people, you may be confused about what's true and what isn't.

SORTING THROUGH THE HYPE

- There are no miracle foods or supplements. Avoid anything that promises rapid results or a quick fix.
- Ignore dramatic statements that go against what most physicians, registered dietitians or national health organizations recommend.
- Stick to what you know about good nutrition, regular physical activity and a healthy lifestyle. Eating a well-balanced diet that includes a wide variety of foods is the best way to obtain the nutrients you need.
- Your best bet is to avoid anything that sounds too good to be true!

Vitamins, minerals and phytochemicals are necessary for good health and provide many great benefits. However, the true benefit comes from food, not from supplements. In a very real way, food is greater than the sum of its parts—you could take all the supplements in the world and still never intake the perfect balance found in food!

While we all know that it's important to eat fruits and vegetables, fewer than 10 percent of adults consume the minimum recommendation of five servings of fruits and vegetables each day. How many servings do you eat? Never substitute other kinds of food for your needed servings of fruits, vegetables and whole grains. Better yet, add a few extra servings and get lots of regular physical activity. When it comes to fruits and vegetables, studies show that eating seven or more servings a day may offer additional health benefits.

ENERGY IN A PILL?

Not likely! Vitamins and minerals do not supply energy—that's the job of calories from macronutrients: carbohydrates, fats and proteins. However, vitamins and minerals play an important part in the process of changing the food you eat into energy your body can use. They're also important for many chemical reactions that take place in your body. The best scientific evidence suggests that your body uses vitamins and minerals best in the combinations found naturally in food.

READ ALL ABOUT IT!

It seems like new information about active natural compounds makes the news every month. You may have heard about antioxidants, omega-3 fatty acids in fish oil, homocysteine and phytochemicals. Here are some brief explanations of what medical science has discovered.

Antioxidants
Three antioxidants are most often in the headlines: beta carotene, vitamin E and vitamin C. Antioxidants help maintain healthy cells by protecting them against oxidation and the damaging effects of free radicals. Free radicals are potentially damaging oxygen molecules that are produced naturally by the body. Some experts believe that environmental factors such as

smoking, air pollution and other stressors increase the production of free radicals. Studies suggest that antioxidants in fruits, vegetables and other foods may help reduce the risk of heart disease, certain cancers and a variety of other health problems. Most experts feel that more studies need to be done before specific recommendations for supplementation can be made.

Fish Oil

Omega-3 fatty acids (ALA, EPA and DHA) have been in the press a lot lately and have even begun showing up on food labels. According to the American Heart Association, omega-3 fatty acids benefit the hearts of healthy people and of those who are at high risk of, or who have, cardiovascular disease. Omega-3 fatty acids reduce the inflammatory effects of certain omega-6 fatty acids (LA, AA), another group of essential polyunsaturated fatty acids. Therefore, a diet rich in omega-3 fatty acids may also prevent other inflammatory diseases such as arthritis, lupus and asthma. Both omega-3 and omega-6 are needed in a healthy diet for normal growth and development, but most Americans eat too little omega-3 and too much omega-6. The balance of the two is what's important.

Omega-6 fatty acids are found in cereals, whole grains, baked goods, vegetable oils, eggs and poultry. Of the omega-3 fatty acids, ALA is found in plant-based foods such as dark greens, walnuts and flaxseed, while EPA and DHA are most prevalent in fish such as salmon, herring, tuna or rainbow trout. Fish-derived oils are the most anti-inflammatory of the omega-3s. Food is always recommended as the best source of nutrients, but because an estimated 25 percent of Americans do not eat fish, many could benefit from supplementing their diet with fish oil capsules.

For more information on supplements, such as how to spot health fraud, visit the National Institutes of Health's Office of Dietary Supplements website at www.ods.od.nih.gov.

In 2004, the U.S. Food and Drug Administration gave "qualified health claim" status to EPA and DHA omega-3 fatty acids, stating that "supportive but not conclusive evidence shows that consumption of EPA and DHA omega-3 fatty acids may reduce the risk of coronary heart disease."[1]

Homocysteine

You may have heard about homocysteine, a protein in the blood. High levels may be associated with an increased risk of heart attack and stroke. Homocysteine levels can be influenced by what you eat. The B vitamins—folic acid, B_6 and B_{12}—help to break down homocysteine in the body. So far, there are no studies showing that taking B vitamins lowers your risk for heart attack and stroke. Everyone should follow an eating plan that has plenty of folic acid and vitamins B_6 and B_{12}. Good sources of these are citrus fruits, tomatoes, dark-green leafy vegetables and fortified cereals and grain products (rice, oats and wheat flour). Eggs, fish, chicken and lean red meats are also good sources.

Phytochemicals

Phytochemicals are substances that plants naturally produce to protect themselves against disease. More than 900 different phytochemicals have been found in plants, and more are being discovered. These same compounds appear to have very beneficial effects on our health as well. You may have heard about some of these: isoflavones, sulphoranes, lycopene and other carotenoids, to name a few. At this time, there is no evidence that these chemicals can be concentrated in pill form to provide health benefits. Take your phytochemicals in the form of fruits, vegetables and whole grains.

QUESTIONS AND ANSWERS

Do I Need to Take Supplements?

The major health organizations such as the American Heart Association, the American Cancer Society or the American Dietetic Association recommend that you get the vitamins, minerals and phytochemicals your body needs from the foods you eat. There's simply not enough information on the dosages or combinations of vitamins, minerals and other nutrients that work best—or work at all! Supplements simply cannot recreate what God has supplied naturally through fruits, vegetables, whole grains and other nutritious foods. Balance these foods with lean meats and fish and low-fat dairy products to get the balance and variety you need for a vitamin-packed eating plan.

What If I'm Already Taking Vitamin and Mineral Supplements?

Taking a multivitamin and mineral supplement that does not exceed the Dietary Reference Intakes (DRIs) is not associated with any harmful effects. Vitamin and mineral supplements can be an important part of an overall health plan if taking them helps you to live a healthier lifestyle— i.e., eating a healthy diet and being more physically active. However, dietary supplements are not a substitute for eating healthy! Vitamin and mineral doses higher than the DRIs should only be taken after seeking advice from your physician or a registered dietitian. For otherwise healthy people, there is only limited data suggesting advantages for taking certain vitamin or mineral supplements in excess of the DRIs.

Are Dietary Supplements More Appropriate for Some People?

Supplements may be appropriate for people in these categories:

- People who have osteoporosis, iron deficiency, digestive disorders and other health conditions may be treated or their conditions prevented with certain dietary supplements.

- People who follow very low-calorie eating plans or restrictive eating patterns (such as a vegetarian who consumes no meat or dairy foods) may need supplements. However, we do not recommend a very low-calorie eating plan.

- People who can't eat certain foods may need a supplement to give their body what it needs. For example, those who are lactose intolerant or have an aversion to dairy foods should strongly consider taking a calcium supplement daily.

- Women planning to become pregnant or who are pregnant or breast-feeding should talk to their doctor about the need for certain supplements such as folic acid and iron.

Note

1. "FDA Announces Qualified Health Claims for Omega-3 Fatty Acids," Food and Drug Administration, September 8, 2004. http://www.fda.gov/bbs/topics/news/2004/NEW01115.html (accessed October 2007).

10 red flags of junk science

I t is an unfortunate reality that not all information is accurate. This is especially true when it comes to weight-loss solutions. New diets are offered on a regular basis, presenting us with the challenge to separate fact from fiction so that we can continue to follow proven, positive steps toward better health. Before you spend money on products that promise fast and easy results, do yourself (and your wallet!) a favor and stop to evaluate if they are truly legitimate claims.

The next time you watch an infomercial, read an advertisement or become hypnotized by the claims of a new "miraculous" weight-loss supplement or diet plan, consider the following list of tips as your measuring stick for credibility. Critically evaluate everything you read, and use your knowledge about what a healthy diet looks like and what it really takes to lose weight and keep it off. (Hint: There is *no* magic pill.) These 10 red flags will help you critique and evaluate such products and programs so that you can spot a scam.

1 **It promises a quick fix.** *"Lose 20 pounds in 2 weeks!"* Face it, permanent weight loss takes time and effort to achieve and maintain. Products that *safely* and *effectively* produce lightning-fast weight loss just don't exist. An average weight loss of 1-2 pounds per week is the safest and most effective way to take off weight and keep it off. It may not be glamorous, but slow and consistent weight loss is your best option.

2 It sounds too good to be true. *"Apply this cream and watch the fat melt away!"* When extravagant claims make the product sound too good to be true, leave it on the shelf and keep moving. If you buy it, the only things you'll lose are money and confidence. Look for telltale words and phrases such as "breakthrough," "miracle," "exclusive," "secret remedy" and "specially formulated."

3 It excludes adopting a healthy diet and regular exercise. *"You'll never need to diet or exercise ever again!"* The formula for weight loss is still the same as it has always been: Burn more calories than you consume. Not only will sedentary programs with unbalanced diet plans prevent permanent weight loss, but they can also seriously compromise your health and well-being.

4 Recommendations are based on a single study. *"A clinical study proved that . . ."* The results of one study only provide one or two pieces of a very large puzzle. Products and programs must be tested several times, in various populations, for different durations and be peer-reviewed by health professionals in order to be deemed credible and without bias. Furthermore, "proof" of cause-and-effect relationships is hardly obtainable from even the most robust of studies. Rather, correlations can be made based on the results of a study, such as "frequent consumption of foods rich in antioxidants *may prevent* different types of cancer." The study should also be published in a reputable medical or health-related, peer-reviewed journal.

5 Simplistic conclusions are made from a complex study. *"Everyone will benefit from this product!"* When things are taken out of context, the resulting message is often blurry and incomplete. Results and conclusions from complex studies often include inherent limitations and bias as well as specific recommendations for specific groups of people. The language of such studies is not broad generalities, so beware of claims that ignore study specifics.

6 **Dramatic statements used to market the product are refuted by reputable scientific organizations.** *"There is no benefit in consuming whole grain foods—cut out all breads."* The American Dietetic Association, American Medical Association, American Cancer Society and the World Health Organization did not become pillars of health education, promotion and research without earning it. Hundreds of health professionals helped build these organizations and continue to pledge their membership by adopting their code of ethics and principles of practice. It is much wiser to heed the advice and findings of these groups than the frail claims of one person or for-profit company.

7 **Foods are divided into the categories "good" and "bad," or a food group is removed completely.** *"Cut out all carbohydrates for the first three weeks."* *"You are allowed to have 'bad' foods on the weekends!"* A single food or meal doesn't make or break a healthful diet. What a person eats over time and how much is eaten are the important things, along with regular physical activity. All foods can fit in a healthy diet, but not all of them should take a prominent place. Also, every food group plays a special role with regard to nutrition; none of them should be vilified or omitted from the diet.

8 **Recommendations are made to help sell a product.** *"Speed up your weight loss with our specially formulated daily supplement."* Unless your personal physician, a registered dietitian or other legitimate healthcare provider has instructed you to add a dietary supplement to your routine, you do not need one. In most cases, the nutrients, vitamins, minerals and active compounds (such as antioxidants) *in foods* are completely sufficient to deliver the nutrition you need. Furthermore, herbal supplements can be dangerous and without benefit. Bottom line: Supplements are highly overused and a big money-maker, so always check with your doctor before using them.

9 **Dire warnings of danger are included with the product or regimen.** *"May cause heart palpitations, nervousness and nausea."* A diet rich in colorful fruits and vegetables, lean meats, fibrous legumes, low-fat and calcium-rich dairy, antioxidant-containing whole grains and healthy oils is without risk to the average adult. So is exercising 30 to 60 minutes a day at a fitness level consistent with your current abilities and goals. Why take a chance with something that is overtly risky when your alternative is exactly the opposite? Consider the risk-benefit ratio of all products or programs.

10 **The person(s) endorsing or selling the product is not a credible health professional in good standing with others in the healthcare community.** *"This program is doctor-approved!"* A person can call himself an expert and wear a white coat without being accredited, bona fide and worth your time and money. Research the credentials of the person you're listening to: To what profession does he or she belong? Is the "professional" as bogus as your weight loss will be?

RESOURCES FOR
THE CONSCIENTIOUS CONSUMER

The Better Business Bureau: www.bbb.org

The Food and Drug Administration: www.fda.gov

The Federal Trade Commission: www.ftc.gov

National Consumer's League Nation Fraud Information Center and Internet Fraud Watch: www.fraud.org

National Council for Reliable Health Information: www.ncrhi.org

the whole story
on whole grains

The 2005 Dietary Guidelines recommend that Americans "make [at least] half their grains whole,"[1] and this equates to a minimum of three 1-ounce servings per day. A 1-ounce serving is:

- 1 slice of 100-percent whole grain bread
- 1 cup of 100-percent whole grain cereal flakes or rounds
- 1 $^1/_4$ cups 100-percent whole grain cereal puffs
- $^1/_2$ cup of 100-percent whole grain hot cereal, cooked pasta, rice or other grain.

Another way to think of this is that a 1-ounce serving of 100-percent whole grains is equal to 16 grams of whole grain. Products offering a half-serving or more of whole grain may contain closer to 8 grams of whole grain per serving. You should aim for at least 48 grams (or three servings of 16 grams) of whole grains per day, if not more! Four, five, even six servings of whole grains each day are not unreasonable—the more servings of whole grains compared to refined grains, the better!

However, most people don't really know what whole grains are, where to find them or how to adopt them into their diet. The health benefits associated with consuming whole grains continue to be documented in the scientific literature, but knowing that they have been shown to reduce the risks of heart disease, stroke, cancer, diabetes and obesity doesn't help you find them in the grocery store. Learn more about what a whole grain really is, why it's beneficial to your health and how to incorporate whole grains into your daily menu.

DEFINITION OF A WHOLE GRAIN

A whole grain is the entire edible seed or kernel of any grain-producing plant: wheat, corn, oats, rice and many others. All grains start out whole. If, after they are processed and refined, they keep all three parts of the original grain—the starchy endosperm, the fiber- and vitamin-rich bran and the small but very nutritious germ—in their original proportions, they still qualify as whole grains.

Often, however, the bran and germ are removed during milling, leaving behind the endosperm, which is used to make white flour. This process yields a product less nutritious than its complete counterpart. Even though manufacturers "enrich" this flour with some vitamins, minerals and fiber, a naturally whole grain product is still the healthier choice.

Simply put, whole grain products retain more protein, fiber, vitamins (such as B vitamins and vitamin E), minerals (such as magnesium, selenium and iron) and antioxidant plant chemicals known as phytochemicals, thus providing a spectrum of important nutrients.

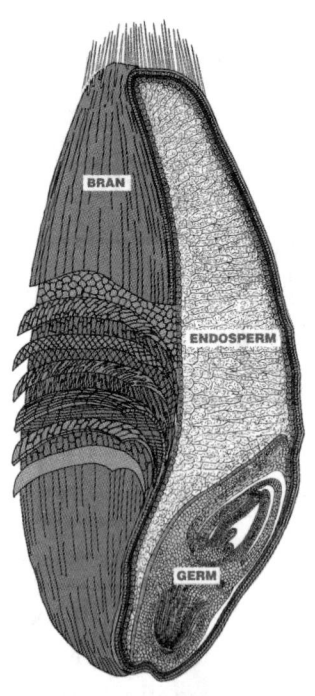

Image courtesy of the Wheat Foods Council

Bran: The outer shell of the seed that contains most of the fiber as well as B-vitamins, trace minerals and phytochemicals. You may have heard of wheat bran or oat bran, which are common ingredients in high-fiber cereals.

Endosperm: The starchy inner body that provides a concentrated source of energy for the young seed to grow as well as smaller amounts of protein, vitamins and minerals. White flour is ground from the endosperm.

Germ: The nutrient-rich portion packed with vitamin E, trace minerals, phytochemicals and essential fatty acids that acts as the baby of the seed, which sprouts into a new plant when pollinated. You may have seen jars of toasted wheat germ in stores, which can be added to a variety of foods to boost nutritional content.

WHOLE GRAINS FOR HEALTH

In the past, fiber and its positive effects on digestive health were considered the primary health benefits of whole grains. However, new research is showing that whole grains contain protective antioxidants and other plant-based nutrients in amounts near or exceeding those in fruits and vegetables! For example, whole grain corn has nearly two times the antioxidants of apples, and wheat and oats almost equal broccoli and spinach in antioxidant activity. (See "Dietary Supplements—Miracle or Myth?" to find out more about the many benefits of antioxidants.)

The strongest recommendation for whole grains to date is for the prevention of cardiovascular disease. Studies have shown that adults who eat at least one to three servings of whole grains a day reduce their risk of developing heart disease by as much as 36 percent.[2] Exact mechanisms have yet to be nailed down as to how

In 1997, the Food and Drug Administration (FDA) authorized the claim that the soluble fiber in oats reduced the risk of coronary heart disease. This approval was extended in 2005 to include the fiber in barley as well.

TYPES OF WHOLE GRAINS

Whole wheat
Wild rice
Brown rice
Buckwheat
Whole grain corn
Whole oats/oatmeal
Barley
Whole rye
Bulgur (cracked wheat)
Popcorn
Millet
Quinoa
Sorghum
Amaranth
Triticale (a hybrid of rye and wheat)

exactly whole grains play a role, but possibilities include their effects on lowering cholesterol and triglycerides, improving insulin sensitivity and protecting cells and tissues from the damage caused by free radicals.

Similarly, studies have also shown that people who consumed a diet rich in whole grains (at least 3 servings per day) were less likely to develop diabetes over the following decade compared to those who ate one serving a week.[3] Reasons for this include how soluble fiber in whole grains such as oats and barley keep carbohydrates from entering the bloodstream too quickly. Filling up on whole grains may also help you maintain a healthy weight. People who consistently eat more whole grains tend to stay more satisfied throughout the day, eat less because of this satiety and tend to have a healthier body mass index (BMI) than those who don't eat many whole-grain foods.

TIPS FOR ADDING WHOLE GRAINS TO YOUR DIET

The easiest way to increase the amount of whole grains you consume is to substitute some processed grain products with their whole-grain equivalents. For example:

- Trade out your white bread for 100-percent whole-wheat bread, or use whole-wheat flour in bread or pancake mixes instead of white flour. Whole-wheat pasta is a delicious substitution and comes in all shapes and sizes. It is prepared the same way as regular pasta but usually needs a few extra minutes to cook. One cup has about 200 calories and 4 grams of fiber!

- Use brown rice with your stir-fry instead of white enriched rice—it has significantly more nutrients such as fiber, selenium and essential fatty acids. Quick-cooking "instant" brown rice, which has been parboiled to speed cooking time, is slightly lower in nutrients than regular, slow-cooking rice, but it still trumps white rice as far as its nutritional value.

▓ Make a whole-grain goodie like oatmeal cookies with raisins for dessert—they're delicious, high in fiber and filling!

▓ When you're at the grocery store, be extra careful when reading food labels. Don't settle for words like "100% wheat," "multigrain," "stone-ground cracked wheat" or "seven grain." These words do not guarantee that the food contains whole grains. Color isn't the best indicator either. Some bread is simply white bread with caramel coloring or molasses added to it. Your best bet is to look at the ingredients list and choose products that have the words "whole [grain such as wheat, oat, barley, rye]" as the first ingredient in the list. Also, look for the "Whole Grain" and "100% Whole Grain" stamps created by the Whole Grains Council in 2005. Below are two examples of stamps you may see on various whole grain products.

Images courtesy of the Whole Grains Council. Whole Grain Stamps are a trademark of Oldways Preservation Trust and the Whole Grains Council (www.wholegrainscouncil.org).

Notes

1. U.S. Department of Health and Human Services and U.S. Department of Agriculture, *Dietary Guidelines for Americans, 2005,* 6th ed. (Washington, D.C.: U.S. Government Printing Office, 2005).
2. "Whole Grains 101," Oldways Preservation Trust/Whole Grains Council, 2003-2007. http://www.wholegrainscouncil.org/whole-grains-101 (accessed October 2007)
3. M. B. Schulze and F. B. Hu, "Primary Prevention of Diabetes: What Can Be Done and How Much Can Be Prevented?" *Annual Review of Public Health,* April 2005, vol. 26, pp. 445-467.

the facts on
fats

L ow-fat," "fat-free," "nonfat," "no fat," "less fat," "reduced-fat"—what do these words mean and is it important to know the difference? Surveys reveal that dietary fat is the number-one nutritional concern of Americans. In fact, for many people, reducing dietary fat has become an obsession. Despite our knowledge about fat and the availability of more low-fat foods, the number of Americans who are overweight or obese is still on the rise—obviously, becoming fats-phobic is not the answer to America's overweight and obesity crisis! Let the following information show you why a better approach is learning about the types of fat and the suggested amounts of fat to include in your diet.

FATS ARE ESSENTIAL FOR GOOD HEALTH!

The importance of fat to your diet is undeniable. Fats are an important source of energy. They supply, carry and store the fat-soluble vitamins—A, D, E and K. Fats are involved in the production of nerve cells, cell membranes and many important hormones. Fats help your body maintain healthy skin and hair. Body fat cushions and insulates the body. Fat also gives certain foods their taste, texture and aroma. Fat satisfies hunger and makes many foods more pleasurable to eat. However, too much fat in the diet (and too much of the wrong kinds of fat) is associated with heart disease, certain cancers, diabetes, obesity and high blood pressure.

HOW MUCH FAT DO I NEED?

The 2005 Dietary Guidelines and Institute of Medicine recommend that 20 to 35 percent of calories for adults come from mostly unsaturated fats. For example, a person who eats 1,800 calories with a total fat intake of 25 percent would consume around 450 calories from fat (or 50 grams of fat) per day. Saturated fat intake, however, should be as low as possible and not exceed 7 to 10 percent of daily calories. Fat contains 9 calories per gram, which is more than twice the calories supplied by carbohydrates and proteins. Because high-fat foods contain more calories, they increase the likelihood of weight gain when their intake is not controlled. However, too many calories from any source and not enough physical activity are the major challenges to weight management. For example, eating low-fat foods high in calories can result in weight gain if you don't monitor portions! Variety, balance and moderation are the keys to a healthy eating plan. Cutting fat without cutting calories or without getting more physical activity will not help you lose weight.

DIFFERENT TYPES OF FAT

All fats are made up of carbon, hydrogen and oxygen molecules and are classified by their chemical structure—saturated, polyunsaturated and monounsaturated. Most foods contain all three types of fats but in different amounts.

Saturated

- Saturated fats have all the hydrogen molecules they can hold. This saturation with hydrogen creates a rigid structure that is solid at room temperature.

- Saturated fats raise blood cholesterol levels more than any other type of fat. Animal foods such as meat, poultry, fish, butter, milk and cheese are high in saturated fats. Coconut oil, palm oil and palm kernel oil are also high in saturated fat.

Polyunsaturated and Monounsaturated

- Polyunsaturated and monounsaturated fats are not saturated with hydrogen molecules because they contain double bonds. This causes them to be flexible and fluid at room temperature. The majority of your fat intake should come from these unsaturated fats, namely healthy oils.

- Polyunsaturated fats (PUFAs) have two or more double bonds and are liquid at room and lower temperatures. They may help decrease blood cholesterol levels when substituted for saturated fats. Based on the position of the double bond, PUFAs come in two types: omega-6 PUFAs and omega-3 PUFAs. Both are *essential* fatty acids, which means that they cannot be made by the body and must be obtained from the diet. Primary sources of omega-6 PUFAs are vegetable oils including soybean, corn oil and safflower oil as well as baked goods, cereals, and eggs and poultry from grain-fed chickens. Primary sources of omega-3 PUFAs are cold-water fish, flaxseed, green leafy vegetables, canola oil, walnuts, and eggs and poultry fed a diet of greens (free-range).

- Monounsaturated fats (MUFAs) have only one double bond, so they remain fluid at room temperatures but begin to solidify in refrigeration. They also help decrease blood cholesterol levels when substituted for saturated fats. Common sources of MUFAs are olive oil, canola oil, peanut oil, almond oil and avocado oil.

CUTTING BACK ON FAT

Because all fats are high in calories (9 calories per gram), cutting back on fat can help you consume fewer calories and lose weight (physical activity helps, too!). The highest sources of dietary fat are found in meats, cheese, eggs, dairy products, desserts, snack foods and nuts. The key to low-fat eating is learning to choose the foods highest in nutrition and lowest in calories—whole grains, fruits, vegetables, lean meats, poultry, fish and low-fat dairy products. Much of the fat in our diet is added: butter, margarine, cheese, oils and salad dressings. Use less of these fats in cooking and preparation. Also, make the switch to low-fat or nonfat alternatives when available. But remember, not all low-fat versions of cakes, cookies or snack foods are low-calorie!

ALL FATS ARE NOT CREATED EQUAL

In terms of calories, all fats add up to 9 calories per gram. However, not all fats are created equal when it comes to health, so it's important to pay attention to the *types* of fat you eat. You're probably aware that diets high in saturated fat and cholesterol are associated with higher levels of blood cholesterol and greater risk for heart disease and certain cancers. But specific fats—in moderation—may have beneficial effects on health. For example, monounsaturated fatty acids in olive and canola oils may increase HDL (good) cholesterol in some people and protect against cardiovascular disease when substituted for saturated fat in the diet. Omega-3 PUFAs have also been shown to lower blood pressure and protect against cardiovascular disease.

Research continues to show that total fat is not necessarily the evil culprit, but rather the *type* of fat consumed. No one is recommending that you increase the total amount of fat in your eating plan, but it is important to shift the balance in favor of the healthier ones—the MUFAs and PUFAs. Specific guidelines for adult fat intake are as follows:

- Total fat: 20 to 35 percent of total calories
- Saturated fat: 10 percent or less of calories for adults with LDL cholesterol below 130 mg/dL and 7 percent or less for adults with LDL cholesterol above 130 mg/dL
- Polyunsaturated fat: 10 percent of calories
- Monounsaturated fat: 10 to 15 percent of calories

EAT LESS SATURATED FAT

Saturated fat is the main culprit when it comes to high blood cholesterol levels. Specifically, eating lots of saturated fat will increase the LDL
cholesterol, which is the bad cholesterol that's linked to fatty buildup in
the arteries. Certain cancers may also be related to higher intakes of saturated fat. That's why it's especially important to limit your intake of
this type of fat.

Meat is where Americans get most of the saturated fat and cholesterol in their diets—although cheese is a close second. Instead of fatty
meats, look for lean cuts of beef and pork, usually labeled "loin" or
"round." And look for lean or extra-lean ground beef, chicken or turkey.
Buy cuts labeled "select" rather than "prime" or "choice." Remove extra
fat and use low-fat cooking methods—grill, boil, broil, bake and roast instead of frying. Look for reduced-fat or fat-free versions of luncheon
meats and hot dogs.

MORE USEFUL TIPS

- Use all fats and oils sparingly, selecting polyunsaturated and
  monounsaturated fats instead of saturated fats (butter, lard,
  shortening and tropical oils—coconut, palm and palm kernel).

- Drink nonfat or low-fat milk (1-percent) and choose low-fat
  or nonfat versions of yogurt and sour cream.

- Learn to modify your recipes with low-fat substitutions.

- Limit the amount of cheese in your eating plan. Choose
  cheeses with 3 to 5 grams of fat per ounce. Use $1/3$ to $1/2$ less
  cheese than a recipe calls for. You can even mix low-fat and
  nonfat versions to cut down on fat and calories. Ounce for
  ounce, cheese is as high in fat and saturated fat as meat!

- Choose low-fat salad dressings and mayonnaise with no
  more than 1 gram of saturated fat per tablespoon. Choose

mustard, ketchup and other low-fat spreads and condiments more often.

▨ Limit the number of eggs you eat each week to two or three. Or substitute two egg whites for every whole egg—the yolks contain most of the fat and cholesterol—or use cholesterol-free egg substitutes.

▨ Use low-fat cooking methods: Make low-fat substitutions in your recipes; sauté using low-sodium broth instead of oils and other fats; chill soups and stews and skim off the fat that collects on the surface.

▨ Cut down on bakery and snack foods—cakes, cookies, pastries, doughnuts and chips. Even low-fat versions can be high in calories!*

HYDROGENATION AND TRANS FATTY ACIDS

You have probably heard about hydrogenation and trans fatty acids in the news over the past few years. But did you know that hydrogenation was patented in 1902 by a German chemist and that by 1911 Procter & Gamble began marketing the first hydrogenated shortening—Crisco—in the U.S.? The process of hydrogenation and its products (trans fats) have been around for quite a while, but in 1992, public health organizations began speaking out about the danger of both.

Hydrogenation is a process that makes unsaturated oils more solid at room temperature (i.e., more like saturated fats). It also reduces rancidity and consequently increases the shelf life of a food. That's why many food manufacturers started adopting the process. Unfortunately, hydrogenation increases the amount of trans fatty acids in a food. The term "trans" simply refers to the geometric configuration of the double bonds on the fat molecule—the building blocks are the same as non-trans fats, but the shape is not. The resulting structure is kinked (as opposed to straight)

* **Note:** Children below the age of two should *not* follow a fat-restricted diet.

and lends itself to plaque formation in the arteries. Trans fatty acids occur naturally in many foods such as meat, butter and milk, but these are consumed less than those produced by hydrogenation and thought to be less dangerous than artificial ones.

You will commonly see the terms "partially hydrogenated" or "hydrogenated" vegetable oil on the label of many processed foods such as margarines, salad dressings, crackers, chips and other baked goods. Try to stay away from these products. The National Academy of Sciences and World Health Organization recommend that trans fats be limited to less than 1 percent of overall calories. Many unqualified claims began surfacing about margarine when the trans fat buzz was high, saying that margarine was worse than butter because it was hydrogenated and contained trans fat. However, many margarines on the market contain 0 grams of trans fat and remain the better choice compared to butter, which is laden with saturated fat and cholesterol, and contains trans fat naturally. Choose margarine that lists liquid vegetable oil or water as the first ingredient, contains no more than 2 grams of saturated fat per tablespoon and is labeled "zero trans fat."

A NOTE ABOUT OMEGA-3 FATTY ACIDS

Both omega-3 and omega-6 fatty acids are essential for health. However, the biological effects of omega-3 and omega-6 fatty acids are largely dependent on their *interactions* with each other. Obtaining the optimum balance of the two is the key issue.

Today, most Americans and people in other industrialized countries get much more omega-6 from their diet than omega-3. A suggested ratio for omega-6 to omega-3 is 4 to 1—most Americans consume a ratio of from 10-to-1 to 30-to-1! Such an imbalance leads to increased inflammation in the body and greater risk of inflammation-related conditions such as asthma, arthritis, lupus and heart disease.

One way to achieve a healthy balance is to eat more fish! A healthy eating plan can include several servings each week. In fact, the American Heart Association recommends that healthy Americans eat fish 2 to 3 times per week and those with existing coronary heart disease eat fish 5

to 7 times per week. Flaxseed, green leafy vegetables, canola oil and walnuts are also good sources of omega-3 fatty acids.

RATING THE OILS

Fats and oils contain a combination of all three types of fatty acids: saturated, polyunsaturated and monounsaturated. All oils are 100-percent
fat and contain 120 calories per tablespoon. The following chart com-
pares fats higher in unsaturated fatty acids (PUFAs and MUFAs) with
those higher in saturated fatty acids:

More Unsaturated:

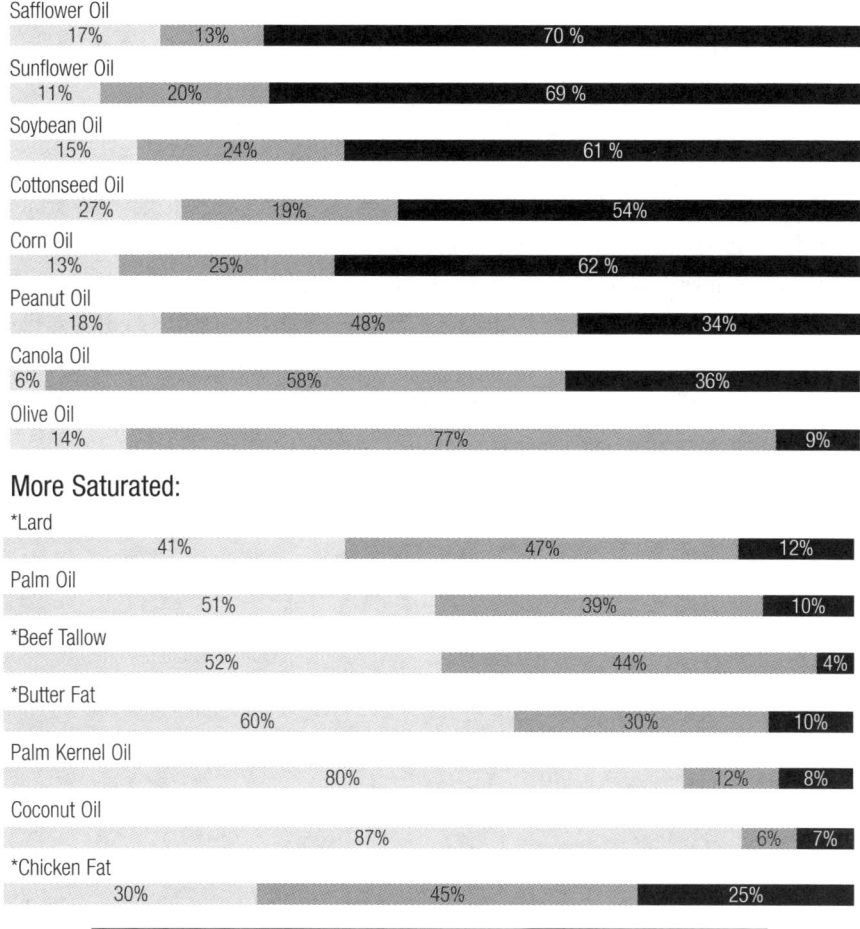

Safflower Oil — 17%, 13%, 70%
Sunflower Oil — 11%, 20%, 69%
Soybean Oil — 15%, 24%, 61%
Cottonseed Oil — 27%, 19%, 54%
Corn Oil — 13%, 25%, 62%
Peanut Oil — 18%, 48%, 34%
Canola Oil — 6%, 58%, 36%
Olive Oil — 14%, 77%, 9%

More Saturated:

*Lard — 41%, 47%, 12%
Palm Oil — 51%, 39%, 10%
*Beef Tallow — 52%, 44%, 4%
*Butter Fat — 60%, 30%, 10%
Palm Kernel Oil — 80%, 12%, 8%
Coconut Oil — 87%, 6%, 7%
*Chicken Fat — 30%, 45%, 25%

% saturated | % monounsaturated | % polyunsaturated | *Animal sources

The following tips are for including fats and oils in a healthy eating plan:

- Stay within the recommended limits for total fat and saturated fat. You may need to cut down depending on your current intake.
- Choose unsaturated sources of fat more often than saturated sources.
- Monitor your portions and limit amounts of both kinds of fat in cooking and preparing foods.
- Choose soft-tub margarine with liquid vegetable oil or water listed as the first ingredient more often than stick margarine (with hydrogenated fats as the first ingredient) or butter.

FAT REPLACERS—FAKE FATS

Fat replacers are added to cheeses, desserts, salad dressings and snack foods to give them the taste and feel of the full-fat versions without the calories. Olestra (OLEAN) is one of the newer fat replacers. It is made from a combination of vegetable fat and carbohydrate. It is calorie-free because it passes through the body without being digested. Olestra appears to be safe; however, it is known to interfere with the absorption of fat-soluble vitamins and to cause digestive discomfort in some people.

Simplesse is a fat replacer found mostly in frozen dairy products. It's made from protein. Although foods made with fat replacers are low in fat, they still have calories and can be low in nutrients.

choosing high-fiber foods!

Many of the foods we eat influence our risk for several diseases, including heart disease, stroke, diabetes and certain cancers. Following an eating plan that is high in fiber and low in saturated fat and cholesterol reduces the risk of these diseases.

High-fiber foods may also help you achieve and maintain a healthy weight, because they fill you up with less fat! Health experts recommend that you eat 14 grams of fiber per 1,000 calories consumed. This usually equates to 21 to 38 grams of fiber per day, depending on your age and sex. The national average for daily consumption is 15 or fewer grams, so you may need to pay close attention to labels at first to make sure you're getting the recommended amount of fiber.

You can get all the fiber you need by making fiber-rich choices more often. For example:

- Choose whole-grain pastas, breads and cereals whenever possible
- Eat whole fruits (fresh, frozen, canned or dried) most of the time instead of drinking fruit juices
- Include legumes—beans, peas and lentils—several times per week

FIBER FACTS

Fiber is found only in the cell walls of plants—fruits, vegetables and grains. Your body does not digest or absorb fiber because humans do not have the necessary enzymes to do so. Therefore, fiber passes from the small intestine into the large intestine relatively intact.

There are two main types of fiber in the diet—*soluble* and *insoluble*. Soluble fiber dissolves in water and forms a gel in the digestive system. The texture of foods like cooked oatmeal comes from soluble fiber. Soluble fiber lowers blood cholesterol levels by blocking the absorption of cholesterol and fats from the diet. In fact, scientists have isolated a component of soluble fiber called beta-glucan that appears to be responsible for many of these benefits. Soluble fiber may also help lower blood sugar, which is significant for diabetics. Good sources of soluble fiber include oatmeal, oat bran, barley, dried beans, peas, brown rice and apples.

Insoluble fiber does not dissolve in water and is more important to digestive health. It provides the roughage that improves bowel function and lowers your risk of colon cancer. Except for being a substitute for foods higher in fat and cholesterol, insoluble fiber does not appear to lower cholesterol levels. Good sources of insoluble fiber are whole-grain breads and cereals, wheat bran and most fruits and vegetables.

The daily recommendation for fiber (21 to 38 grams) includes both soluble and insoluble fiber.

DIETARY FIBER AND WEIGHT CONTROL

Both types of fiber may help in weight control. High-fiber foods are more filling and less fattening (that is, they are usually lower in calories and fat). Also, eating meals that are high in fiber—meals that include fruits, vegetables, whole grains and legumes—leaves less room for foods that are high in calories and fat. Don't go overboard, however: Very high-fiber, low-calorie diets are not good ways to lose weight because they come up short in other important nutrients. Fiber supplements are also not recommended for weight loss. Balance, moderation and variety are the keys to good nutrition!

Getting Enough Dietary Fiber

Look at the nutrition facts label and choose items with at least 2.5 to 4.9 grams of fiber per serving. These are *good* sources of fiber. Foods offering 5 or more grams of fiber per serving are considered *excellent* sources of fiber. The following table can steer you toward more fiber in your diet.

FOOD	SERVING	FIBER (in grams)	SOLUBLE	INSOLUBLE
White bread	1 slice	Less than 1		
Wheat bread	1 slice	Less than 1		
White rice	1/2 cup	Less than 1		
Refined pasta	1/2 cup	Less than 1		
Graham crackers	2 squares	2		✓
Broccoli	1/2 cup	2		✓
Orange	1 medium	2		✓
Whole-wheat bread	1 slice	2 to 3		✓
Whole-grain bread	1 slice	2 to 3		✓
Whole-wheat pasta	1/2 cup	2 to 3		✓
Bran muffin	1 medium	2 to 3	✓	✓
Oat, oatmeal	3/4 cup	3	✓	✓
Apple with skin	1 medium	3	✓	✓
Brown rice	1/2 cup	3 to 4	✓	✓
Potato with skin	1 medium	3 to 4	✓	✓
Legumes and peas	1/2 cup	4 to 6	✓	✓
Bran cereal	1/2 cup	6 to 15	✓	✓

INCREASING THE FIBER IN YOUR DIET

- Choose more whole- or multigrain breads. Look for whole-wheat or whole-grain flour as the first ingredient.
- Start your day with a bowl of whole-grain or bran cereal.

- Try adding $1/4$ cup of wheat bran to foods such as cereal, pancakes, applesauce, yogurt or meat loaf.
- When baking, substitute whole-wheat flour for half of the white flour called for in the recipe.
- In baked goods, substitute oats for one-third of the flour called for in the recipe.
- Mix at least one-half refined pasta with whole-grain pasta or white rice with brown rice in dishes.
- Increase your intake of beans, lentils, soybeans and peas. Use them instead of meat in casseroles or other dishes.
- Add legumes, wheat bran or other grains to soups, pasta, salads and other dishes.
- Leave the skin on fruits and vegetables such as apples, pears, peaches and potatoes.
- Add fresh or dried fruits to cereals and salads.
- Add extra vegetables to salads, soups and other dishes.
- Read food labels. Foods with 2.5 or more grams of fiber per serving are good sources of fiber, as are foods with 20 percent or more Percent Daily Value (%DV) for fiber. Foods offering 5 or more grams of fiber per serving are considered excellent sources.

outsmarting
the snack attack!

I t's not snacking that's bad; it's the usual snack choices—chips, crackers, dips, cookies, candy bars, and so on—that are the problem! The truth is that your body works best when it refuels every four to six hours. The best way to fuel your body is to eat light, well-balanced meals and two or three healthy snacks per day. Snacking may even help you lose weight by taming your appetite, thus preventing the tendency to overeat and make poor choices. Learn to make *healthy* snacks a part of your daily eating plan, and hold the guilt!

FIRST THINGS FIRST

Why do you snack? Do any of the following reasons sound familiar?

- To satisfy hunger
- To satisfy cravings
- To relax
- For enjoyment and pleasure
- To fight boredom and pass time
- For nourishment
- To boost energy
- For emotional comfort

Some of these reasons are perfectly acceptable; others may signal deeper issues to explore. Use snacks to satisfy hunger, nourish your body, boost your energy and help you reach your goals for a healthy weight. Pay attention to how your typical snack foods stack up nutritionally.

HEALTHY SNACKING

The key to healthy nutrition is variety, balance and moderation. With these principles in mind, snacking can be an important part of a healthy eating plan. Snack time can be a great way to get in your daily servings of fruits, vegetables and whole grains. Low-fat dairy foods such as milk and yogurt also make healthy snacks. Keep a supply of healthy snacks in convenient locations. Concentrate on whole-grain and high-fiber carbohydrates and low-fat proteins. Do whatever you can to avoid those high-fat, high-sugar treats that always seem to show up at home, work and social occasions. Healthy beverages can also be great at snack time—water, fruit or vegetable juice and low-fat milk are your best choices.

HEALTHY SNACK CHOICES
(~50 Calories Each)

30 small pretzel sticks	8 celery ribs	6 cherry tomatoes
1 tangerine	4 saltine crackers	$3/4$ cup consommé or
2 tomatoes	2 fortune cookies	broth
1 cup zucchini sticks	2 cups broccoli florets	12 whole radishes
1 large dill pickle	1 kiwi fruit	1 caramel popcorn cake
1 (4-inch) rice cake	3 apricots	2 slices garlic crisp bread
1 cup tomato juice	$1/2$ cup blueberries	$1/2$ cup mandarin orange
1 carrot	10 ripe olives	slices
2 gingersnaps	$1/2$ cup orange juice	$1/4$ cup tropical fruit salad
$3/4$ cup raspberries	1 medium cucumber	
12 strawberries	4 slices melba toast	
$1/2$ cup fat-free milk	1 medium peach	

The important thing to remember about snacking is that *when* you eat is not as important as *what* and *how much* you eat. When it comes to weight control, the issue is total calories—not when or how often you eat. As for when, the only rule is to eat only when you're hungry and stop when you're full!

HOW COMMON SNACKS STACK UP

SNACKS	CALORIES	FAT
Ice cream (1 cup)	~ 300	~ 15 grams
Candy bar (2 ounces)	~ 250	~ 12 grams
Mixed nuts (1 ounce or 20 nuts)	~ 200	~ 15 grams
Fried chips (1 ounce or 10 chips)	~ 160	~ 10 grams
Microwave popcorn (3 cups)	~ 150	~ 10 grams
Nonfat fruit yogurt (1 cup)	~ 120	0 grams
Baked chips (1 ounce or 13 chips)	~ 110	~ 1 gram
Pretzels (1 ounce or 9 pretzels)	~ 110	~ 1 gram
Fresh fruit (1 medium)	~ 60	trace
Air-popped popcorn (3 cups)	~ 50	trace
Vegetable (1/2 cup)	~ 25	trace

PLAN AHEAD

Stock your home, office and workout bag with a variety of healthy snacks so that you'll always have something healthy on hand when hunger strikes. Buy several plastic containers, plastic bags, a thermos and an insulated lunch bag or cooler to make it easy to carry snacks with you. Keep a special shopping list to help you remember to stock up on healthy snack foods. Instead of looking for low-fat versions of your favorite processed snack foods, choose foods such as whole-grain breads and crackers, fruits, vegetables, rice cakes and low-fat yogurt.

SNACK FACTS

How much do we spend on snacking? Sales of candy, the largest snack food category, garnered $19.9 billion in 2005.[1] Salty snacks brought in $11.7 billion.[2] In a study released in June 2004, junk foods such as sugary sodas and chips were found to make up nearly one-third of calories consumed by average Americans.[3] On the positive side, many of our favorite snack foods now come in low-fat versions. Unfortunately, many of these are still high in calories and low in nutrition.

Notes

1. "Snack Food Trends in the U.S.," Packaged Facts, 2006. http://www.marketresearch.com (accessed October 2007).
2. Ibid.
3. "Block G. Foods Contributing to Energy Intake in the US: Data from NHANES III and NHANES 1999-2000," *Journal of Food Chemistry and Analysis*, June 2004, (17):439-447.

sweetness by any other name

Many different sugars are found naturally in foods. They are also added in the preparation and manufacturing of many processed foods. In addition to tasting good, sugar plays several important roles: It gives certain foods their characteristic texture, color and consistency. You may have discovered the difference that sugar makes when you reduce or substitute it in recipes.

Myths and misinformation about sugar and other sweeteners are very common. Common table sugar, or refined sugar, tops the misinformation list. You've probably also heard stories about saccharin and aspartame. The big picture is that whether the sugar comes from the sugar bowl, honey, fruit, vegetables or milk, there's little difference from your body's viewpoint. In the end, your body converts sugars and starches from fruits, vegetables, grains and other foods to glucose. Along with fatty acids (fat), glucose is the main energy source for your body.

THE TRUTH ABOUT SUGAR

A gram of sugar contains 4 calories. That's not bad, considering it's less than half of the 9 calories supplied by a gram of fat. However, if a teaspoon of sugar (which is equal to 4 grams) contains 16 calories and a typical soft drink contains 9 to 12 teaspoons of sugar, what's the real problem? Answer: the quantity!

The bottom line is that too many calories are fattening, and it doesn't really matter whether the extra calories come from sugar, fat or protein. We gain weight when we take in more calories from our food than we expend in physical activity.

The problem with sugar is that it often supplies empty calories—that is, calories without the nutrition. Sugar is also frequently found in foods that are high in calories and fat. Because many of us have a sweet tooth, sugary foods often replace more nutritious foods in our diets.

SOURCES OF SUGAR

Acesulfame K	Glucose	Molasses
Aspartame	Honey	Saccharin
Brown sugar	Lactose	Sorbitol
Corn sweeteners	Maltose	Sucralose
Dextrose	Mannitol	Sugar
Fruit-juice concentrate	Maple syrup	Xylitol

While there are some minor differences in these sources of sugar, your body treats them the same. In terms of nutritional value, there's virtually no difference. The non-nutritive sweeteners in this table—acesulfame K, aspartame and saccharin—add sweetness without the calories.

THE SKINNY ON SWEETENERS

Non-nutritive sweeteners (also known as artificial, or intense, sweeteners) can give you the taste of sugar without the calories. It's important to read product labels; many foods labeled "sugar-free" contain a sugar substitute, or non-nutritive, sweetener. Even though foods made with non-nutritive sweeteners may be low in calories, many of them may also be low in nutrition. In a healthy eating plan, calories are not the only issue—you need to consider nutrition (vitamins, minerals, phytochemicals and fiber). However, non-nutritive sweeteners offer greater variety and flexibility for people wanting to reduce their caloric intake *and* satisfy their sweet tooth.

Five artificial sweeteners are commonly used today: aspartame, acesulfame K (potassium), saccharin, polyols or sugar alcohols, and sucralose.

1 **Aspartame** (NutraSweet™ and Equal™) is a newer non-nutritive sweetener that contains some calories. It's actually a combination of two amino acids. Because it's 180 times as sweet as sugar, you need only a tiny amount to sweeten food. One problem with aspartame is that it loses its sweetness when heated. Consequently, you can't use it in baked goods, such as cakes. You can use it in top-of-the-stove foods like pudding by adding it at the very end of cooking. The safety of aspartame has been confirmed by the regulatory authorities in more than 100 countries, including the U.S. Food and Drug Administration, the Joint Expert Committee on Food Additives of the World Health Organization and Food and Agriculture Organization, and the European Commission's Scientific Committee on Food.

2 **Acesulfame K** (Sunett™) is 200 times sweeter than sugar and was first approved in 1988 as a tabletop sweetener. It is now approved for products such as baked goods, frozen desserts, candies and beverages. More than 90 studies verify its safety. It is often combined with other sweeteners. Worldwide, the sweetener is used in more than 4,000 products, according to its manufacturer, Nutrinova. It has excellent shelf life and does not break down when cooked or baked.

3 **Saccharin** (Sweet'N Low™) has been around for more than 100 years. It's more than 300 times sweeter than table sugar—a little goes a long way! Saccharin can be used in both hot and cold foods to make them sweeter. However, substituting saccharin for sugar in baked goods may change taste, texture and appearance. The risk of cancer associated with the use of saccharin in laboratory animals appears to be very low or non-existent in humans.

4 **Polyols or Sugar Alcohols** (Mannitol and Sorbitol) are a group of low-calorie sweeteners that deliver the taste and texture of sugar with half the calories. They are often used to replace sugar, cup for cup, in many sugar-free and low-calorie foods. Polyols vary in sweetness from about half as sweet as sugar to equally sweet. They are frequently combined with small amounts of other low-calorie sweeteners. Since polyols are only partially absorbed in the body, over-consumption may cause laxative effects similar to that of prunes, beans or certain high-fiber foods, so consume them only in moderate amounts.

5 **Sucralose** (Splenda™) is 600 times sweeter than sugar and is made from sugar. A small amount of chlorine is added during the manufacturing process, which changes the structure of the sugar molecule to yield a calorie-free sweetener. Chlorine is present naturally in many foods we eat every day such as lettuce, mushrooms and table salt. First discovered in 1976, sucralose was approved in 1998 for use in products such as baked goods, beverages, gum, frozen dairy desserts, fruit juices and gelatins. In 1999, it was approved as a general-purpose sweetener for all foods. Because it is granular, it pours and measures like sugar. It has a good shelf life and doesn't degrade when exposed to heat, so it can be used for cooking and baking. The safety of sucralose has been documented by a thorough safety evaluation program and more than 100 studies conducted over a 20-year period.

A NOTE ABOUT STEVIA

Stevioside (Stevia) is one of the newest sweeteners on the scene. It is actually an herb in the sunflower family that has been used for centuries by native peoples in Paraguay and Brazil. It is about 200 to 300 times sweeter than sugar and can be purchased in many local natural food stores.

However, just because something is "natural" doesn't mean that it should automatically be considered safe. Currently, the FDA allows Stevia to be imported as a dietary supplement but not as a food additive, because its safety has not yet been proven. This means that individuals may choose to use Stevia as a supplement (supplements are not regulated by the FDA), but it has not been approved as a sweetener in mass production (for example, in diet sodas).

In contrast to the other sweeteners mentioned above, little research has been conducted to determine the effects of Stevia in various amounts. Many other health organizations have banned the use of Stevia in foods until further data are published, including the World Health Organization (WHO), the European Union (EU) and the Canadian Food Inspection Agency (Canada's equivalent to the FDA).

> **SOFT DRINKS: HARD ON THE DIET**
>
> The What America Drinks report, published in 2007, revealed that nearly 50 percent of people aged 4 and older consumed an average of 24-ounces of regular soft drinks on any given day, which provided 36% of all added sugars in their diets.[1] A 20-ounce cup of Coke contains a hefty 16 teaspoons of sugar and a whopping 256 calories! Buyer beware: These calories are "empty," which means they provide no nutrition and can add up quickly if you're not careful.

THE WISE USE OF SUGAR

Moderation, balance and variety are the keys to achieving and maintaining a healthy weight and good nutrition. Some dietitians actually advise people trying to lose weight to include some sugary foods in their diets because eating plans that restrict certain foods are often too hard to maintain. Trying to eliminate certain foods often leads to an eventual slip-up, when you break down and eat that food. Slip-ups often lead to feelings of guilt and failure. These feelings cause many people to abandon their weight-loss efforts. Others report that there are certain foods they need to avoid in order to achieve their goals. Only you can decide what is best for you and your body.

There are no good or bad foods, only bad diets. Your eating plan should not focus on what you are eliminating but what you are adding: good nutrition, improved health and a higher quality of life.

Note

1. "What America Drinks" is a comprehensive analysis of U.S. beverage consumption that was conducted by ENVIRON International Corporation. The report analyzed data from more than 10,000 Americans aged 4 years and older who participated in the government's National Health and Nutrition Examination Survey (NHANES) in 1999-2000 and 2001-2002 and provided reasonable dietary reports of food/beverage intakes. Relationships between selected patterns of beverage use, nutrient intakes and body mass index (BMI) were examined.

the truth about
fad diets!

Lose Weight Without Exercising!
Take Off Pounds While You Sleep!
Lose 30 Pounds in 30 Days!
Zap 3 Inches from Your Thighs!

Doesn't it seem as if there's always a new miracle diet or supplement being advertised or reported in the media? One of the biggest reasons people give for not starting or sticking with a healthy eating plan is confusion and frustration over all the conflicting information.

It is estimated that Americans spend more than $46 billion each year on products and plans to lose weight.[1] Despite all the money people spend, two-thirds of them regain the weight lost within a year; and an estimated 98 percent of individuals who lose weight gain it back within five years, according to the National Institutes of Health.[2]

A NEW, OLD APPROACH

Have you ever tried a diet or supplement that promised more than it could deliver? Why didn't these programs or products work for you?

Because there is no diet, pill or product that can produce the benefits that come with following God's plan for healthy living. You are truly "fearfully and wonderfully made" (Psalm 139:14). The secret to good health and effective living is deciding to care for your body as God's good creation (see 1 Corinthians 6:19-20). Are you ready to commit to a healthy lifestyle of good nutrition and regular physical activity?

PLAN EVALUATION

Remember, no food, diet or product provides all the magic answers for good health or weight loss. To help you sort through the confusion, use the following quick-reference guidelines when evaluating information:

- Does the program promise a quick fix?
- Do the claims sound too good to be true? (Watch out for the words "breakthrough" or "miracle.")
- Does the program include regular physical activity?
- Are only certain foods or products emphasized? Are other foods off-limits?
- Do you have to buy special supplements or products?
- Does it seem impossible to follow the program for a lifetime?
- Does the program go against the recommendation of major nutrition, medical and scientific organizations?

If you answered yes to any of the questions above, leave the fad diet on the shelf and stick to what is validated by credible professionals.

THE FACTS ABOUT FAD DIETS

Most fad diets are recycled every few years with a few new twists added to make them seem different. Fad diets are usually unbalanced and don't provide the variety you need for good health or enjoyable eating. *A calorie is a calorie*, whether it comes from fat, protein or carbohydrate. You gain weight when you take in more calories than your body needs. Here are some common types of fad diets to watch for.

Instant Success Through Miracle Supplements

Many fad diets take advantage of people's desire for instant results by creating the myth that certain foods or supplements have special physiologic or metabolic properties for quick weight loss. There are no known miracle foods or supplements that burn fat or promote long-term weight loss.

A loss of one to two pounds per week is all the body can healthfully lose. More rapid weight loss is the result of water loss, not fat loss. Over the long term, some of these diets will even result in muscle loss—especially if physical activity is not involved.

Combining Foods to Boost Metabolism

Some fad diets suggest that eating foods in certain combinations will help you burn fat more effectively, boost your metabolism or improve your health. These diets, like the ones that promote miracle foods, don't work! God did not design eating to be a complicated affair.

Digestion is an amazing process that uses specific enzymes in specific areas of your digestive track. Combinations of certain foods, timing of meals or special supplements do not have any effect on this process. Another problem with these diets is that they don't provide the variety and balance your body needs for good health.

Weight Loss Without Exercise

Most fad diets don't encourage physical activity. In fact, some programs promise weight loss while you sleep! Physical activity should be one of the highest priorities of any weight-loss program. Few people can maintain long-term weight loss without regular physical activity. Besides that, we need physical activity to keep healthy and prevent disease.

Guaranteed to Work for Everyone

Avoid diets that offer a one-size-fits-all approach. There is no one diet that works for everyone. Weight regulation is a complex process that involves many factors. A good weight-loss program considers individual needs and differences. A good program allows you to personalize your eating plan. You are more likely to stick to a plan that most closely reflects your lifestyle, tastes and preferences.

Over-the-Counter Products

Fad diets may offer easy access to over-the-counter weight-loss drugs or supplements. Studies show that even approved weight-loss medications result in a weight loss of only 10 to 15 percent; it's unlikely that a product advertised in the back of a magazine or on the side of the road will be any more effective. Some of these supplements may even cause serious side effects—even death! Never take medication or a supplement without talking to your primary doctor.

Packaged Program Foods

Many diet programs sell packaged foods. These products may make a lot of money for the commercial programs, but they may not be the most effective way to teach people how to develop and follow a healthy eating plan. To be effective, a weight-loss program must teach people how to develop *lifelong* habits of healthy eating and regular physical activity. This includes learning how to choose and prepare healthy foods.

FIND A CREDIBLE SOURCE

The most reliable spokespersons to help you lose weight have training in nutrition and medicine from reputable universities. Registered dietitians (RDs) are the best source for credible nutrition information. To find a local dietitian in your area, ask your physician for a referral, contact the American Dietetic Association or visit their website at www.eatright.org.

"Experts" and Celebrity Endorsements

Many programs are sold by self-proclaimed experts who make sensational claims and are promoted using personal success stories of famous television, film or sports celebrities. When you check the "credentials" of these so-called experts, you'll find very few who are respected in the medical community. And don't think for a minute that your favorite celebrity is supporting that product for free just because he or she loves it! Endorsements are a big-money business.

Notes

1. C. L. Bish, H. M. Blanck, M. K. Serdula, et al, "Diet and Physical Activity Behaviors Among Americans Trying to Lose Weight: 2000 Behavioral Risk Factor Surveillance System," *Obesity Research*, 2005, (13):596-607.
2. J. S. Stern, J. Hirsch, S. N. Blair, et al, "Weighing the Options: Criteria for Evaluating Weight-management Programs. The Committee to Develop Criteria for Evaluating the Outcomes of Approaches to Prevent and Treat Obesity," *Obesity Research*, November 1995, 3(6):591-604.

understanding
vitamins and minerals

I f you're like most people, you probably have many questions about vitamins and minerals: Do I need to take supplements for good health? If so, which ones do I need? How much is too much? Do supplements contain what they say they do? Who and what should I believe?

The Food and Nutrition Board of the National Academy of Sciences and the Institute of Medicine continually updates its recommendations on vitamins and minerals as better scientific knowledge becomes available. You may hear about Dietary Reference Intakes (DRIs), Recommended Dietary Allowances (RDAs), Adequate Intake (AI) and the Tolerable Upper Intake Level (UL).

All of these terms can get confusing, but here's what you need to know in brief. RDAs are the dietary intake amounts that meet the nutritional requirements of nearly all healthy individuals so as to prevent deficiency. DRIs are values that estimate nutrient intake amounts to be used for planning and assessing diets for healthy people and include levels of certain nutrients that may reduce the risk of cardiovascular disease, osteoporosis, certain cancers and other diet-related diseases. Over the next few years, DRIs will replace RDAs, and the emphasis will shift from preventing deficiency to decreasing the risk of chronic disease through nutrition.

The UL is the maximum safe level of a nutrient that is likely to pose no risk of adverse health effects. The term "tolerable upper limit" was chosen to communicate that no possible beneficial effect of consuming more can be achieved. As intakes of a nutrient increase above the UL, the risk for adverse effects increases. AI is a value assigned to nutrients that do not have an RDA as a goal for individuals to achieve.

The following tables will help you gain a better understanding of vitamins and minerals—what they do, how much is recommended (DRIs), common doses in supplements, UL when available and, most important, the best food sources. The tables reflect dosages for healthy adults who are 18 and older.

VITAMINS

There are 13 vitamins. Four of them are fat-soluble (A, D, E and K), and nine are water-soluble (C and the B vitamins). Compared to the major nutrients—carbohydrates, fats, proteins and water—vitamins are only needed in small amounts, and they are not a source of energy for the body.

Please note: It is advised that you discuss the issue of vitamin and mineral supplementation with your personal physician. These charts are for informational purposes only.

	ROLES AND FACTS	DRI	NATURAL AND DIETARY SOURCES
VITAMIN A	Maintains healthy cells, skin and bones; important for vision and immune function. High doses can damage the liver. It's easy to get all the vitamin A you need from a healthy diet.	Women: 700 micrograms (mcg); Men: 900 mcg. UL is 2,800 to 3,000 mcg.	Dairy products (cheese, butter, egg yolks); liver; fish oil; fortified foods; and dark-green, yellow and orange vegetables.
BETA-CAROTENE (CAROTENOIDS)	Beta-carotene from plant sources is converted to vitamin A. Beta-carotene is an antioxidant that may protect the body from heart disease, cancer and cataracts.	No DRI—Supplements range from 2,500 to 25,000 international units (IU) (1.5 to 15 mg).	Look for fruits and vegetables with orange, red, yellow or dark green color (carrots, sweet potatoes, spinach, red bell pepper, apricots, mangoes and cantaloupe).

	ROLES AND FACTS	DRI	NATURAL AND DIETARY SOURCES
VITAMIN C	An antioxidant that protects your body's cells. Important for healthy skin, connective tissue, bone and immune function. Large doses may increase the risk of kidney stones.	60 mg—Supplements range from 60 to 500 mg. Women: 75 mg; Men: 90 mg. UL is 2,000 mg.	All citrus fruits, cantaloupe, straw-berries, tomatoes, red and green bell peppers, potatoes and broc-coli.
VITAMIN D	Helps your body absorb cal-cium and phosphorous and build healthy bones. Too much vitamin D can cause kidney damage and weaken bones.	Men and women: 5 to 15 mcg (200 to 600 IU). Supplements range from 100 to 800 IU. UL is 50 mcg (2,000 IU).	Vitamin D is formed by the action of sunlight on the skin. Most milk products are fortified. Eggs, fish, margarine and fortified cereals also contain vitamin D.
VITAMIN E	An antioxidant that protects your body's cells. It may protect against heart disease and can-cer. It's been *claimed* to cure almost anything and to slow the aging process.	Men and women: 15 mg (22 in natural source, 33 in synthetic source). UL is 1,000 mg (1,500 in natural source; 1,100 in syn-thetic). Supplements range from DRI to 400 IU.	Vegetable oils, nuts, seeds, salad dressings, margarine, wheat germ and green leafy vegetables.
VITAMIN K	Important for blood clotting; a de-ficiency of vitamin K is very un-likely because your body produces it from bacteria in the intestines, and it is abundant in food.	Women: 90 mcg; Men: 120 mcg. No need to supplement.	Green leafy vegetables such as spinach and broccoli, peas, eggs, meat, milk, cereal and fruits.
THIAMIN (VITAMIN B1)	Important for energy produc-tion, metabolism and building healthy cells such as proteins, blood and nerves.	Women: 1.1 mg; Men: 1.2 mg. Appears to be nontoxic.	Whole grains, fortified cereals, en-riched grains, nuts, seeds and meats.
RIBO-FLAVIN (VITAMIN B2)	Important for energy produc-tion, metabolism and building healthy cells such as proteins, blood and nerves.	Women: 1.1 mg; Men: 1.3 mg. Appears to be nontoxic.	Whole grains, fortified cereals, en-riched grains, nuts, seeds, meats, dairy products and green leafy vegetables.
NIACIN	Important for energy produc-tion, metabolism and building healthy cells such as proteins, blood and nerves.	Women: 14 mg; Men: 16 mg. UL is 35 mg.	Same as riboflavin—meats are the best source.
VITAMIN B6 (PYRIDOXINE)	Important for energy produc-tion, metabolism and building healthy cells such as proteins, blood and nerves. Reduces lev-els of homocysteine, which is associated with heart attack and stroke. High doses can cause nerve damage.	Women: 1.3 to 1.5 mg; Men: 1.3 to 1.7 mg. Supplements range from DRI to 50 mg. UL is 100 mg.	Same as riboflavin.

	ROLES AND FACTS	DRI	NATURAL AND DIETARY SOURCES
FOLATE	Important for energy production, metabolism and building healthy cells such as proteins, blood and nerves. Very important in pregnancy for the prevention of birth defects; reduces levels of homocysteine, which is associated with heart attack and stroke.	400 mcg. UL for supplementation is 1,000 mcg.	Same as riboflavin; legumes and fortified cereals are important sources.
VITAMIN B12	Important for energy production, metabolism and building healthy cells such as proteins, blood and nerves. Reduces levels of homocysteine.	2.4 mcg. Appears to be nontoxic.	Animal and fortified foods only.
BIOTIN	Essential for activity of many enzyme systems.	30 mcg. Supplements range from 30 to 100 mcg. Appears to be nontoxic.	Found in a wide variety of foods, including liver, egg yolk, milk and yeast.
PANTO-THENIC ACID	Critical in metabolism and synthesis of carbohydrates, proteins and fats.	5 mg. Appears to be nontoxic.	Found in a wide variety of foods, including whole grains and eggs.

MINERALS

	ROLES AND FACTS	DRI	NATURAL AND DIETARY SOURCES
CALCIUM	Necessary for healthy bones. Plays an important role in muscle and nerve function and in blood clotting. Low calcium intake increases the risk for osteoporosis. High calcium intake can cause kidney stones.	1,000 to 1,200 mg. Aim for 1,200 mg. Supplements range from 250 to 1,500 mg. UL is 2,500 mg.	Milk and dairy products (yogurt and cheese); dark-green leafy vegetables; fortified foods such as juice and some cereals. Tofu and soy milk are also good sources.
CHLORIDE	Helps regulate fluid balance; important in digestion and nerve function.	1.8 to 2.3 g. No need to supplement. UL is 3.6 g.	Salt
CHROMIUM	Works with insulin to regulate blood sugar. Studies don't support its role in promoting weight loss.	Women: 20 to 25 mcg; Men: 30 to 35 mcg. Supplements range from 50 to 200 mcg. Appears to be nontoxic.	Meat, eggs, whole grains and cheese.

	ROLES AND FACTS	DRI	NATURAL AND DIETARY SOURCES
COPPER	Important in red blood cell formation and is a part of many enzyme activities.	900 mcg. Supplements range from 1 to 3 mg. UL is 10,000 mcg.	Seafood, nuts and seeds.
FLUORIDE	Important for healthy bones and teeth.	Women: 3 mg; Men: 4 mg. Supplements range from 1.5 to 4 mg. UL is 10 mg.	Fluoridated drinking water and seafood.
IODINE	An important part of thyroid hormone, which regulates metabolism.	150 mcg. UL is 1,100 mcg.	Salt, seafood and some vegetables.
IRON	Needed to carry oxygen in the blood.	Women: 8 to 18 mg; Men: 8 mg. UL is 45 mg. Avoid taking supplements with high doses of iron unless prescribed by doctor.	Meats (the redder and darker the meat, the higher the iron), fortified cereals and grains, beans, nuts, seeds and dried fruits.
MAGNESIUM	Important for healthy bones, nerves and muscles; a component of many enzymes.	Women: 310 to 320 mg; Men: 400 to 420 mg. UL is 350 mg.	Legumes, nuts, whole grains and leafy green vegetables.
MANGANESE	A component of many enzymes.	Women: 1.8 mg; Men: 1.3 mg. Supplements range from 2 to 5 mg. UL is 11 mg.	Whole grains, fruits and vegetables and tea.
MOLYBDENUM	A component of many enzymes.	45 mcg. Supplements range from 75 to 250 mcg. UL is 2,000 mcg.	Milk, legumes and whole grains
PHOS-PHOROUS	Important for healthy bones and teeth—helps regulate energy and maintain healthy cells.	700 mg. UL is 3,000 to 4,000 mg.	Dairy products, meats, legumes, nuts and eggs.
POTASSIUM	Helps regulate fluid balance and is important in muscle and nerve function.	4.7 g. Supplements may contain 2,000 mg.	Seafood, meats and eggs; grains, nuts and seeds.
SELENIUM	An antioxidant that protects body's cells. May be protective against some cancers.	55 mcg. UL is 400 mcg.	Seafood, meats and eggs; grains, nuts and seeds.
SODIUM	Helps regulate fluid balance; important in muscle and nerve function. A diet high in sodium may promote high blood pressure.	1.2 to 1.5 g. No need to supplement. Limit to 2,300 mg/day.	Table salt and processed foods.
ZINC	Important for cell growth, immune function, wound healing and energy metabolism.	Women: 8 mg; Men: 11 mg. UL is 40 mg.	Meat, seafood, whole grains, nuts, seeds, milk and eggs.

SUMMARY AND CAUTIONS

Try to meet your body's need for vitamins and minerals by following a healthy eating plan. If you and your doctor decide that taking a supplement is right for you, talk to your physician about his or her recommendations, and stay within the dosages listed in these tables.

The dosages listed in these charts pertain to adults. Separate recommendations exist for children and adolescents.

If you're pregnant, breast-feeding or thinking about becoming pregnant, discuss your nutritional needs with your personal physician. Separate recommendations exist for pregnant and lactating women.

The above common dosages may not apply to elderly individuals or people with underlying health problems. If you think you may have special nutritional needs, talk with your personal physician before taking any vitamin or mineral supplements.

choosing better beverages

The old saying about drinking at least eight glasses of water a day needs a few additional sentences in order to clear up confusion and address some details. Read on to learn about the importance of water, how much you need, where to get it and why it is a great beverage choice when wanting to lose weight.

THE IMPORTANCE OF WATER

Water makes up about 75 percent of your brain, 80 percent of your muscle mass, 60 percent of your red blood cells and more than 90 percent of your blood plasma. If you were stranded on a deserted island, you could go for weeks without food but only a few days without water. Take a look at the important role water plays in your body.

- Your metabolism works more efficiently when you are hydrated, so water aids in the digestion and absorption of foods and nutrients.
- Water helps regulate the chemical reactions in every cell of your body.
- It transports nutrients and oxygen.

- It is the vehicle your body uses to flush out the waste produced in normal body functions.
- It helps you maintain normal body temperature.
- Water is necessary for proper bowel function.
- It is responsible for maintaining proper fluid balance.

In your quest for healthy living, don't forget to give your beverage choices ample consideration. The water and water-based beverages that you'll learn more about in the following pages definitely fall into the "better" category.

HOW MUCH DO YOU NEED?

The National Academy of Sciences considers adequate intakes (AI) of total daily water for men and women 19 years or older to be 3.7 and 2.7 liters, respectively. In fact, national survey data shows that healthy women consume an average of 91 ounces (about 11 cups or 2.7 liters) of total water each day and healthy men average 125 ounces (about 16 cups or 3.7 liters) daily.[1]

What most people don't know is that all fluids and some foods count toward your daily total water intake. Your hydration and total water needs for the day can be met by a variety of sources in addition to drinking water. In fact, about 80 percent of your total water intake comes from drinking beverages, including caffeine-containing beverages, with water in food providing the other 20 percent.

Contrary to popular belief, there is no convincing evidence that caffeine leads to anything but temporary water loss. You should still watch your caffeine intake and limit it to less than 400 milligrams daily (less than 300 milligrams for pregnant and breastfeeding women).

HEALTHY BEVERAGE BREAKDOWN

Your body loses about 8 to 12 ounces of water throughout the day. To stay healthy and feel your best, you need to replace what your body loses. Drinking water and water-based beverages throughout the day helps you keep ahead of the game.

Simple or Flavored Water

Most beverages count toward your total daily water, but water is the only fluid that the body truly *needs*. Your taste buds may ask for alternatives now and again, but since water contains no calories, is low in sodium and contains no additives or stimulants, it definitely should not be replaced altogether! Nowadays you can select calorie-free and sugar-free drink mixes to add to water for flavor and a little variety. Aim for 4 to 8 cups of water if you plan to include other beverages, and consume additional water (8 to 12 cups) if you limit other beverages.

Unsweetened Coffee and Teas

Research has shown that coffee may provide some health benefits and tea provides a variety of flavonoids and antioxidants that may prevent chronic disease such as certain cancers. Both contain caffeine, so monitor your intake (see recommendation above). If you do sweeten your coffee or tea, use a conservative amount of sugar (remember 1 teaspoon equals 16 calories) or artificial sweetener.

Low-fat (1-percent) or Skim (fat-free) Milk and Unsweetened Fortified Soymilk

Milk is a rich source of calcium, magnesium and potassium readily absorbed by the body. Through fortification, it is also a good source of vitamin D. For the lactose intolerant or vegan, fortified soymilk is a great alternative with many of the same benefits. Also, did you know that 1-percent and skim milk are both about 90 percent water? Since 2-percent and whole milk contain a significant amount of calories, fat and saturated fat, they are not

---

TOTAL DAILY WATER NEEDS EXPLAINED

The current recommendation for *total* daily water is 2.7 liters for women and 3.7 liters for men. This includes the water in your beverage *and* food choices. If 80 percent of your total water needs typically come from beverages, this means you need to drink:

72 ounces of fluid (about 9 cups)
   if you're a woman
2.7 liters x 0.80 = 72 ounces

100 ounces of fluid (about 12 cups)
   if you're a man
3.7 liters x 0.80 = 100 ounces

The remaining 20 percent of your total daily water needs should come from "juicy foods" such as fruits, vegetables, meats and soups.

recommended and should be considered "seldom" beverages. Sweetened or flavored low-fat milk products contain the same nutrients but come with additional calories due to the added sugars. Aim for 1 to 3 cups of low-fat or skim milk per day, depending on your intake of other calcium-rich foods.

100-Percent Fruit and Vegetable Juices

These juices provide various nutrients but lack fiber and some of the nutrients found in whole fruits and vegetables. By focusing on fruits and varying your vegetables, you can easily obtain the benefits from a diet rich in these foods without including juice. Many fruit juices contain added sugars, and vegetable juices often contain added sodium—an issue you don't face with either when in their natural state. If you do choose to drink juice, limit your intake to 1 to 2 servings per day and always look for varieties low in added sugar and sodium.

Sports Drinks

These beverages were designed for endurance athletes who need to replace electrolytes, sodium, chloride and potassium lost during endurance events. Choose these drinks very sparingly if you are not currently participating in any endurance activities (strenuous activity lasting 60 to 90-plus minutes).

OTHER BEVERAGES

Calorie-Free, Artificially Sweetened Beverages

These include things like diet sodas and other artificially flavored drinks, teas and coffees. Even though the Food and Drug Administration (FDA) has approved at least five artificial sweeteners as safe food additives, some research suggests that adults who frequently drink diet drinks tend to have a higher preference for sweets.

Caloric, Sweetened Beverages Without Nutritional Benefits

These include regular soft drinks, fruit drinks like fruit punch, and sweetened teas and coffees. These beverages are higher in calories with little (if any) nutritional benefits. Caloric sweeteners like sugar and high-fructose corn syrup have been linked to poor dental health, excess calorie consumption, weight gain and Type 2 Diabetes. These drinks should be limited as much as possible. With all the other beverage options available, you should find no problem substituting these calorie-dense, nutrient-lacking beverages if you resolve to do so!

TAP OR BOTTLED?

Americans drink about 7.5 billion gallons of bottled water each year, which translates into an average of 26.1 gallons per person, and the numbers have been increasing about 10 percent per year. In 2003, bottled water emerged as the second most popular beverage category (behind carbonated soft drinks).[2] There are some 475 bottled water plants in the United States, producing 600 brands of bottled water.

If drinking water from a bottle will encourage you to drink more, then bottled water is a good choice. However, don't assume that it's purer than tap water. In fact, according to the Natural Resources Defense Council (NRDC), some bottled waters may not be any better than tap water—they may even *be* tap water! In a recent study, the group found that one-third of 103 tested brands contained bacteria or other chemicals that exceeded the industry's own guidelines or state purity standards.[3]

While bottled water is safe, the NRDC noted that bottled-water companies tout the health benefits of their products and that consumers should be getting their money's worth. Since the study was released, legislation has been proposed for stricter standards on bottled water. Tap water is regulated under provisions of the Safe Drinking Water Act of 1974.

TIPS TO HELP YOU CHOOSE MORE WATER

- Fill a pitcher with water and add several orange slices for a light, refreshing flavor.
- Ask for water when dining out even if you are drinking something else. Ask for slices of lemon or lime for a naturally sweet and tangy flavor!

- Try sparkling waters.
- Buy water bottles with pop tops. They're easier to carry around and use than twist-off caps.
- Keep a water bottle in your car.
- Take a water break at work!
- Drink a glass of water an hour or so before dinner. Not only will you get some water in, but you'll also help control your appetite and prevent overeating.
- Keep water bottles in the fridge for easy access.

DEHYDRATION

During the summer, your body requires more water because it loses more water through perspiration. If you live in a dry climate, your perspiration may evaporate quickly and you might not sense the need to drink water, even though your body is losing fluids. (Dry air in winter also increases your body's need for water.) Don't wait for perspiration to be your warning sign to consume more water. Remember to stay ahead of your thirst.

In addition to thirst, early signs of dehydration include the following:

- Fatigue
- Loss of appetite
- Flushed skin
- Light-headedness and dizziness
- Muscle cramping
- Infrequent urination and urine that is dark yellow

WATER AND PHYSICAL ACTIVITY

During physical activity, pay close attention to your water intake. Make sure you drink at least 8 ounces before activity and every 15 to 20 minutes during activity. You may need more when it's hot outside. To find out how much water you need to replenish your exercise losses, weigh yourself before and after exercise—the difference is mainly water. Replace 1 pound of weight loss with 16 ounces of water.

While the number on the scale may look better, dehydration is not a healthy way to lose weight. Avoid using sweat suits or rubberized clothing to increase sweating during exercise. This is a dangerous practice, and the weight you lose is only water—not fat! Body fat is made up of only 25 percent water compared to muscle, which is almost 80 percent water. Dehydration robs your body of the water it needs to build muscle and strength.

ESSENTIAL FOR SURVIVAL

Next to air, you need water most for survival. Keep well hydrated and your body will perform better than ever!

Unless you are an endurance athlete training for more than an hour, drink water rather than sports drinks.

WHERE'S THE FLUORIDE?

The FDA began allowing bottled water companies to promote fluoridation in 2006, a decision that received wholehearted support from the American Dental Association (ADA). Bottled water containing between 0.6 and 1.0 mg/L total fluoride can make the claim that drinking fluoridated water may reduce the risk of dental cavities or tooth decay. The ADA recommends that children over age one who drink bottled water most of the time should drink the fluoridated variety.

Notes

1. "Dietary References for Water, Potassium, Sodium, Chloride and Sulfate," The National Academies, February 2004. http://www.nap.edu.
2. "Bottled Water: More Than Just a Story about Sales Growth," International Bottled Water Association, April 13, 2006. http://www.bottledwater.org/public/2006_Releases/2006-04-13_bev mkt.htm.
3. "Bottled Water: Pure Drink or Pure Hype?" The National Resources Defense Council. http://www.nrdc.org/water/drinking/bw/chap2.asp.

controlling cholesterol

Today, almost everyone knows something about cholesterol. In fact, many people know their most recent blood cholesterol numbers. However, with what seems like a new report on cholesterol every day, it's easy to become overwhelmed.

Believe it or not, cholesterol is important for good health. It is used to make certain hormones, it helps digest fat and it's an essential part of every cell membrane. Your blood cholesterol levels are influenced by several factors: heredity, diet, physical activity, body weight and other life-style habits.

The foods you eat can have a big impact on your blood cholesterol level. Eating foods high in saturated fat and cholesterol can raise your cholesterol level. Too much cholesterol in the bloodstream increases the chances that your blood vessels will become blocked with fats, cholesterol and other components. This blockage can lead to heart attack and stroke.

DID YOU KNOW?

- Cholesterol is not a fat—it's a fatlike substance called a "sterol."

- Saturated fat raises blood cholesterol levels more than dietary cholesterol does.

- Cholesterol is found in animal products, not in plant foods. Saturated fat, however, is found in some plant foods, including palm oil, palm kernel oil and coconut oil.

- The body makes all the cholesterol it needs; it's not necessary to get cholesterol from food.

- Children younger than two years of age should not follow a low-fat, low-cholesterol eating plan. Fat and cholesterol are necessary for normal growth and development and a healthy nervous system.

UNDERSTANDING CHOLESTEROL LEVELS

When most people talk about their cholesterol level, they're talking about total cholesterol. The higher your total cholesterol, the higher your risk for heart disease. However, there's more to blood cholesterol than the total level.

Cholesterol is carried in your body in special packages called *lipoproteins*. The two most important lipoproteins are *LDL* cholesterol and *HDL* cholesterol. Think of the *L* in LDL as standing for *lousy*. This is the bad cholesterol that tends to block arteries. People who have too much LDL have a higher risk of heart disease. Think of the *H* in HDL as standing for *helpful*. HDL is the good cholesterol that carries cholesterol away from the arteries. People who have a high level of HDL have a lower risk of heart disease.

You may also have heard about *triglycerides*. In your body, fat is carried in the bloodstream in the form of triglycerides. Triglycerides and cholesterol are often carried together in the same packages. High blood triglycerides levels appear to be associated with an increased risk of heart disease in some people.

CHECK YOUR LEVELS

Don't wait until you retire to have your cholesterol tested for the first time. The American Heart Association recommends getting it tested beginning at age 20 and then having it retested every five years. The most accurate results can be obtained when your weight has been stable for at least two weeks and you are following a consistent diet.

KNOW YOUR NUMBERS

Do your cholesterol levels meet these recommended levels?

1. Total cholesterol less than 200 mg/dL

   ❏ Yes ❏ No

2. LDL cholesterol less than 130 mg/dL (less than 100 mg/dL if you have any risk factors for heart disease)

   ❏ Yes ❏ No

3. HDL cholesterol higher than 40 mg/dL (for men) or higher than 50 mg/dL (for women)

   ❏ Yes ❏ No

4. Triglycerides less than 150 mg/dL

   ❏ Yes ❏ No

Did you answer no to any of these? If so, you may have abnormal cholesterol levels. If you have abnormal blood cholesterol levels—in particular, high LDL cholesterol—experts agree that lowering your blood cholesterol can reduce your risk of having a heart attack and certain kinds of strokes. Talk to your doctor about what's best for you. If you don't know your numbers or you haven't had your cholesterol checked in several years, make an appointment with your doctor for a checkup.

YOUR LOW-CHOLESTEROL LIFESTYLE

Everyone needs to follow an eating plan that's low in fat, saturated fat and cholesterol, and high in whole grains, fruits and vegetables. It is also important to achieve and maintain a healthy body weight—losing weight lowers cholesterol levels. Physical activity is important because it raises the good HDL cholesterol and helps you maintain a healthy weight. Smoking, on the other hand, lowers HDL levels.

CHOOSE	INSTEAD OF
Lean meats, poultry and fish with visible fat and skin removed	Fatty cuts of meat, organ meats (liver, kidneys) or other high-fat meats (sausage, bacon)
3 to 6 ounces of meat each day (3 ounces is about the size of a deck of cards)	Typical restaurant-sized portions of 8 to 12 ounces
Fat-free or low-fat milk or yogurt, and some low-fat cheese	Reduced fat (2-percent) or whole milk and full-fat yogurt, cheese or cheese spreads
Soft margarine that lists liquid vegetable oil or water as the first ingredient and contains no hydrogenated oils or trans fat	Stick butter or margarine that lists hydrogenated vegetable oil as the first ingredient and contains trans fats
Vegetable oils (canola, olive, safflower, corn) and low-fat salad dressings or mayonnaise	Shortening, tropical oils (palm and coconut), mayonnaise or full-fat salad dressings
Low-fat cooking methods: broil, bake, grill, roast or poach	Frying or cooking with heavy creams, cheese and sauces
More fruits, vegetables and whole grains every day	Meat and highly processed breads, cereals and snack foods

COUNTING CHOLESTEROL AND SATURATED FAT

Use the following table to compare the cholesterol, saturated fat and total fat in various foods. Limit the cholesterol in your diet to less than 300 mg per day. If you have heart disease, stay under 200 mg per day.

CHOLESTEROL AND
SATURATED FAT COMPARISONS

	TOTAL FAT (g)	SATURATED FAT (g)	CHOLESTEROL (mg)
Liver (3 ounces, cooked)	4	2	333
Eggs (1 whole)	5	2	213
Shrimp* (8 medium)	2	1	167
Hamburger (3 ounces, cooked)	17	8	77
Lean beef (3 ounces, cooked)	8	3	72
Baked, skinless chicken breast (3 ounces, cooked)	3	1	72
Whole milk (1 cup)	8	5	33
Natural cheddar cheese (1 ounce)	9	6	29
Glazed doughnut (1 medium)	10	2	18
Skim milk (1 cup)	1	trace	4
Whole-wheat bread (1 slice)	1	trace	0
Fruits and vegetables, except avocados and olives	trace	trace	0

* Shellfish such as shrimp were once considered off-limits because of their high cholesterol content. However, because they're low in saturated fat, they can be a heart-healthy choice—but not if dipped in batter and fried!

preventing cancer

Scientific evidence suggests that at least one-third of cancer deaths are related to dietary factors. In fact, experts predict that for the majority of Americans who don't smoke, dietary and physical activity habits are the most important modifiable risk factors for cancer—though a definitive answer about the optimal diet for preventing cancer and which nutrients have specific effects is not yet known.

WHAT IS CANCER?

Cancer is a group of diseases caused by the abnormal growth and spread of the body's cells. When these cells grow out of control, they can develop into cancerous (malignant) tumors. Cancers result in death by interfering with the body's normal processes.

Many factors contribute to cancer, including heredity, aging, environment and lifestyle. We know from cancer-related statistics that tobacco smoke causes more than 8 out of 10 cases of lung cancer.[1] A woman with a mother, sister or daughter with breast cancer has twice the risk of developing breast cancer as do women who do not have such a family history.[2] Overexposure to the sun's rays increases the risk for skin cancer.

To prevent cancer and cancer deaths, early detection and eliminating risk factors are critical.

CANCER AND NUTRITIONAL HEALTH

Several groups publish nutrition guidelines to advise the public about dietary practices that reduce the risk of cancer. Current recommendations are based on the consensus of hundreds of experts and thousands of scientific studies. The following are consistent with dietary recommendations from the American Cancer Society, National Cancer Institute, World Cancer Research Fund and the American Institute for Cancer Research:

- **Choose most of the foods you eat from plant sources.** Eat at least five servings of fruits and vegetables each day (five to nine servings is the current recommendation). Try to choose dark green and yellow vegetables, vegetables in the cabbage family, soy products and legumes. Eat at least three servings of whole grains daily including breads, cereals, rice and pasta.

- **Limit your intake of high-fat foods, particularly those from animal sources.** Select lean cuts and smaller portions when you eat meat, use low-fat cooking techniques, select nonfat or low-fat dairy products and replace high-fat foods with fruits, vegetables, grains and legumes.

- **Get 30 minutes or more of moderate-intensity activity on most days of the week.**

- **Achieve and maintain a healthy weight.**

- **Limit consumption of alcoholic beverages to two drinks for men and one for women.**

DID YOU KNOW?

About half of all cancer deaths are related to tobacco use, unhealthy diet, physical inactivity and being overweight or obese.

SCIENTIFIC EVIDENCE ON FOODS AND BEHAVIORS THAT PROTECT

- Fruits and vegetables contain many beneficial vitamins, minerals, fiber and phytochemicals (plant chemicals) that may protect against cancer. Some of the nutrients that may be specifically beneficial include the antioxidant vitamins, fiber, calcium, folate, selenium, carotenoids, flavinoids and sulfurophanes. Studies show that an increased consumption of fruits and vegetables reduces the risk of certain types of cancer. The evidence is particularly strong for colon cancer.

- High-fat diets, particularly saturated fats, are associated with an increased risk of cancers of the breast, colon and prostate; and possibly cancers of the rectum, ovary, endometrium (uterus) and pancreas.

- Consumption of meat, particularly red meat, has been associated with certain cancers. What's the best advice? Limit meat intake to the recommended servings and portion sizes (3 to 6 ounces); choose lean cuts of meat, poultry (without the skin), fish and meat alternatives such as legumes instead of high-fat red meats; and avoid charring meat over a direct flame.

- Physical activity may help protect against cancer of the colon, breast, prostate and endometrium. The protective effects may be related to energy balance and hormone levels.

- Maintaining a healthy weight is a significant preventative measure.

- Excessive intake of alcoholic beverages is associated with an increased risk of cancer in the oral cavity, esophagus, larynx and breast.

THE BENEFIT OF WHOLE GRAINS

When data from 40 recent studies on whole grains and cancer risk were analyzed, risk for cancer was reduced by 34 percent on average in people who ate large amounts of whole grains compared to those who ate small amounts.[4]

CANCER SCREENING

Cancer screening is one of the most important steps to increase your chances of surviving cancer. Regular screening examinations are currently recommended for the breast, cervix, colon, oral cavity, prostate, rectum, testes and skin. Self-examination of the breast, testes and skin are important steps in detecting cancer early. A regular medical checkup can also detect cancers of the thyroid, lymph nodes, ovaries and other areas of the body. Here is a cancer-related checkup schedule recommended by the American Cancer Society.[5]

Breast
Monthly self-examination should begin at age 20, with clinical examinations every three years for women ages 20 to 40, then yearly after age 40. The American Cancer Society recommends yearly mammograms beginning at age 40 and continuing for as long as a woman is in good health.

Cervical
All women should have a yearly Pap test and pelvic examination about three years after they begin having sexual intercourse, and no later than age 21; then a regular Pap every year or every two years using the liquid-based Pap test.

Colon and Rectum
Regular screening of the colon and rectum should begin at age 50 (if you have a strong family history of colon cancer or polyps, you may need to begin screening earlier). Tests usually involve a yearly examination for blood in the stool and a rectal examination. Every 5 to 10 years, one of the following tests to look at the inside of the colon should also be performed: a sigmoidoscopy, a colonoscopy or a barium enema. Talk to your doctor about the screening test and schedule that is best for you.

Prostate
Beginning at age 50, men should have yearly digital rectal examinations and Prostate-Specific Antigen (PSA) blood tests. African-Americans and

men with a strong family history of cancer may want to begin screening at age 45. Men at even higher risk, with multiple relatives affected at an early age, should consider a screening at age 40. Talk to your doctor about what's best for you.

Notes

1. "What Causes Non-small Cell Lung Cancer?" American Cancer Society, August 10, 2006. http://www.cancer.org/docroot/CRI/content/CRI_2_2_2x_What_Causes_Non-small_Cell_Lung_Cancer.asp?sitearea= (accessed October 2007).
2. K. McPherson, C. M. Steel and J. M. Dixon, "Breast Cancer–Epidemiology, Risk Factors and Genetics," *British Medical Journal*, September 9, 2000, 321(7261):624–628.
3. "American Cancer Society Report Finds Drop in Total Cancer Deaths," American Cancer Society, February 9, 2006. http://www.cancer.org/docroot/MED/content/MED_2_1x_American_Cancer_Society_Report_Finds_Drop_in_Total_Cancer_Deaths.asp (accessed October 2007).
4. World Cancer Research Fund/American Institute for Cancer Research, *Food, Nutrition, Physical Activity and the Prevention of Cancer: A Global Perspective* (Washington, D.C.: AICR, 2007.)
5. "American Cancer Society Guidelines for the Early Detection of Cancer," American Cancer Society. March 28, 2007. http://www.cancer.org/docroot/PED/content/PED_2_3X_ACS_Cancer_Detection_Guidelines_36.asp (accessed October 2007).

preventing
diabetes!

D iabetes is a serious disease and is the sixth leading cause of death in the United States, according to the U.S. Centers for Disease Control and Prevention. Nearly 21 million Americans have diabetes, and one in three don't even know they have it! Each year, nearly 1.5 million people are diagnosed and more than 224,000 deaths result from diabetes. Diabetes and its complications kill more Americans each year than breast cancer and AIDS combined. Diabetes is very damaging to the body and is a major cause of blindness, kidney disease, nerve damage and amputations. In fact, people with diabetes have two to four times the risk of heart attack and stroke.[1]

TYPES OF DIABETES

Diabetes means that your blood sugar—glucose—is too high. Your blood always has some sugar in it because your body requires a constant supply of sugar for energy. However, too much sugar in the blood is not good for your health.

Most of the food you eat is converted into glucose—sugar—for energy. For the glucose to get into the body's cells, a hormone called insulin must be present. In a person who has diabetes, either the body does not produce enough insulin or the cells don't use it properly. As a result, blood-sugar levels rise. There are two major types of diabetes.

Type 1

Type 1 diabetes is an autoimmune disease in which the body does not produce enough insulin. It usually begins in childhood or young adulthood. Without enough insulin, the body cannot control blood sugar. The only way to survive with Type 1 diabetes is to take daily injections of insulin. Type 1 accounts for only 5 to 10 percent of all diabetes sufferers.

Type 2

Type 2 diabetes results from an inability to make enough insulin or to properly use it—insulin resistance. Type 2 is the most common form of diabetes and accounts for 90 to 95 percent of cases. This form of diabetes usually develops in adults over the age of 45; however, it is on the rise among children and adolescents. Nearly 85 percent of people with Type 2 diabetes are overweight. Type 2 diabetes is on the rise due to the increasing age, weight and sedentary lifestyles of Americans.

RISK FACTORS FOR TYPE 2 DIABETES

Doctors don't yet understand all the reasons that people develop Type 2 diabetes. The following factors (many of which can be lowered with healthy lifestyle habits) are associated with a higher risk:

- Family history of Type 2 diabetes in a parent or sibling
- Overweight and obesity
- A sedentary lifestyle
- A history of diabetes during pregnancy or delivery of a baby weighing more than nine pounds
- Low HDL cholesterol ($\leq$ 35 mg/dL) or high trigycerides ($\geq$ 250 mg/dL)
- High blood pressure ($\geq$ 140/90)

- African-Americans, Latino Americans, Native Americans, Asian Americans and Pacific Islanders have a higher risk than other ethnicities

DIAGNOSIS OF DIABETES

Experts now recommend that all adults 45 years and older be tested for diabetes. If you're under 45 years of age and you have one or more risk factors for diabetes, you should also be tested. Early diagnosis and treatment can lower the risk of the serious complications associated with diabetes. The best way to test for diabetes is to have a blood test performed after you haven't eaten anything for at least eight hours. This is called a fasting plasma glucose test. Do you know your blood sugar level?

RISK CLASSIFICATION	FASTING PLASMA GLUCOSE LEVEL	MY LEVEL
Normal	< 99 mg/dL	
Increased Risk (pre-diabetes)	100 to 125 mg/dL	
Diabetes	≥ 126 mg/dL	

If your blood glucose is normal, take lifestyle steps to keep it that way and undergo repeat testing every three years. If your level puts you at an increased risk, ask your doctor about further testing and what lifestyle adjustments you can make to decrease your risk. If you have diabetes, you must take your blood sugar levels very seriously. Work with your doctor and a registered dietitian to do all you can to keep your blood sugar under control.

PREVENTION OF DIABETES

There are several things you can do to lower your risk for Type 2 diabetes. If you're at risk, it's important that you do all you can to prevent diabetes. Fortunately, following a healthy lifestyle will help keep your risk low. In addition to living a healthy lifestyle, make sure to get regular medical checkups.

- **Follow a healthy eating plan.** Healthy eating can help to keep your risk low. A healthy eating plan is high in fruits, vegetables and whole grains, and low in foods that are high in total fat, saturated and trans fat, and cholesterol.

> ## A MATTER OF LIFE AND DEATH
>
> According to a recent study, the typical American has a one in three chance of developing Type 2 diabetes. It's not a disease to ignore: Diabetes can shorten a person's lifespan by 10 to 15 years.[2]

- **Control your weight.** Weight gain is associated with increasing risk for diabetes—the higher your weight, the higher your risk. If you're overweight, a weight loss of as little as 5 to 10 percent can significantly reduce your chances of developing diabetes.

- **Exercise regularly.** A sedentary lifestyle and low level of physical fitness is associated with an increased risk for developing diabetes. Regular physical activity and exercise help your body use insulin and sugar more efficiently. Physical activity also helps you achieve and maintain a healthy weight and lowers your risk for heart disease. Are you doing at least 30 minutes of physical activity several days each week?

Notes

1. "National Diabetes Fact Sheet," Centers for Disease Control, November 16, 2005. http://www.cdc.gov/diabetes/pubs/estimates05.htm (accessed October 2007).
2. K. M. Venkat Narayan, J. P. Boyle, T. J. Thompson, et al, "Lifetime Risk for Diabetes Mellitus in the United States," *Journal of the American Medical Association,* 2003, (290):1884–1890.

preventing heart disease

You probably have a loved one who has come face to face with some form of cardiovascular disease, which refers to diseases of the heart and blood vessels. Nearly one in three adults has some form of heart disease. Cardiovascular disease claims approximately 650,000 lives in the United States each year and is the leading killer of both men and women. Nearly 1.2 million heart attacks occur each year and some 450,000 result in death—and more than one-half of these victims are women! Stroke, another form of cardiovascular disease, is the third leading killer of men and women.[1]

THE CAUSES OF HEART ATTACKS AND STROKES

Arteriosclerosis is the underlying process that causes most heart disease. It is the buildup of fat, cholesterol and cells in the lining of the arteries. This buildup is called *plaque*, and as it progresses, the flow of blood to the heart or brain can be blocked or the plaque can rupture, causing a heart attack or stroke. While a heart attack or stroke can occur suddenly, arteriosclerosis develops as a result of many years of unhealthy choices.

THE NINE MAJOR RISK FACTORS

There are now nine major risk factors for heart disease, according to the American Heart Association. The more factors a person has, the greater the risk of heart attack and stroke. Notice that the first three are factors that cannot be changed, but the rest can be avoided by making lifestyle changes.[2]

1 Increasing age. More than 83 percent of people who die of coronary heart disease are age 65 or older, says the American Heart Association. At older ages, women who have heart attacks are more likely than men to die from them within a few weeks.

What is your age? _____

2 Gender. Men are more likely to have heart attacks than women, and they typically have them earlier in life. Women's death rate from heart disease increases after menopause; however, it's not as great as men's.

What is your gender? _____

3 Heredity (including race). Your risk is higher if you have a family history of heart disease. In addition, heart disease risk is higher among African Americans, Mexican Americans, Native Americans, native Hawaiians and some Asian Americans. Note that most people with a strong family history of heart disease have one or more other risk factors.

Do you have a family history of heart disease?

❑ Yes   ❑ No

4 Smoking. A smoker's risk of developing heart disease is two to four times that of a nonsmoker. Secondhand smoke also increases your risk. A smoker is much more likely to die when a heart attack or stroke occurs than a nonsmoker. If you smoke, make every possible effort to quit.

Are you currently a smoker?

❏ Yes   ❏ No

5 **Abnormal cholesterol levels.** The risk of heart disease rises as the total and LDL (bad) cholesterol levels increase. The risk of heart disease also rises as HDL (good) cholesterol levels decrease. High triglycerides may also increase your risk.

What are your cholesterol levels?
Write your levels in the appropriate boxes.

RISK	LOW		BORDERLINE HIGH		HIGH	
	RANGE	MY SCORE	RANGE	MY SCORE	RANGE	MY SCORE
Total cholesterol	< 200		200-239		≥ 240	
LDL cholesterol	<100		130-159		160-189	
HDL cholesterol	≥ 60				<40 in men, <50 in women	
Triglycerides	< 150		150-199		200-499	

If your numbers are in the high or borderline-high range and you have two or more other risk factors, you may be greatly adding to your risk of a heart attack or stroke. Talk to your doctor. Treatment and prevention always involve lifestyle changes such as following a diet low in saturated fat and cholesterol, achieving and maintaining a desirable weight and exercising regularly.

6 **High blood pressure.** High blood pressure increases the risk of heart attack and stroke. A blood pressure greater than 140/90 is high. Even pressures slightly lower—120-139/80-89—can put you at greater risk, according to the American Heart Association.

What is your blood pressure?
Write it in the appropriate box.

RISK	NORMAL	BORDERLINE	HIGH
Scale	< 120/80	120-139/80-89	≥ 140/90
My Blood Pressure			

If your blood pressure is high or unusually low, talk to your doctor. Treatment and prevention for high blood pressure always involve lifestyle changes such as weight control, physical activity and restriction of alcohol and sodium intake. An eating plan high in fruits and vegetables (7 to 10 servings) and low-fat dairy products (2 to 3 servings) may also help lower blood pressure.

7 **Physical inactivity.** A sedentary lifestyle increases the risk of heart disease nearly two times. This risk is as high as that caused by abnormal cholesterol levels, high blood pressure *and* cigarette smoking combined. Despite the known risks, more than half of adults don't get enough physical activity to benefit their health. Regular moderate physical activity cuts your risk of dying from heart disease in half.

Are you getting at least 30 minutes of moderate physical activity several days each week?

❏ Yes ❏ No

8 **Obesity and overweight.** Excess body fat increases the risk for both heart attack and stroke. Obesity is also associated with increased blood pressure, abnormal cholesterol levels and diabetes. Losing just 10 percent of excess weight and keeping it off can significantly lower risk.

THE STRESS CONNECTION

A person's response to stress may be a contributing factor to heart disease. A person under a great deal of stress may overeat or start smoking—factors putting them at great risk for heart disease.

Are you within your healthy weight range?

❏ Yes ❏ No

9 Diabetes. Type 2 diabetes (high blood sugar) is very damaging to the heart and blood vessels. If you or a loved one has diabetes, it's important to do all you can to control blood sugar and other risk factors. A fasting blood sugar level of 100 to 125 mg/dL signals pre-diabetes, and a level greater than 125 mg/dL indicates diabetes.

What is your fasting blood sugar level? _____

Notes

1. A. M. Miniño, M. P. Heron, S. L. Murphy and K. D. Kochankek, "Deaths: Final Data for 2004," *National Vital Statistics Reports*, vol. 55, no. 19 (Hyattsville, MD: National Center for Health Statistics. 2007.)

2. "Risk Factors and Coronary Heart Disease, AHA Scientific Position," American Heart Association. http://www.americanheart.org/presenter.jhtml?identifier=4726 (accessed October 2007).

preventing
osteoporosis

Osteoporosis is one of the most significant health problems in the U.S. Some 10 million Americans, mostly postmenopausal women, are estimated to have osteoporosis—and another 34 million have low bone mass, putting them at risk for the disease, says the National Osteoporosis Foundation. Osteoporosis results in more than 1.5 million fractures each year. Unfortunately, many of these fractures in elderly people result in significant disability—even death![1] The seriousness of osteoporosis makes low calcium intake one of the most important nutrition-related problems in the country. A sedentary lifestyle is also a major risk factor.

WHAT IS OSTEOPOROSIS?

Osteoporosis is a weakening of the bones that results from the gradual loss of calcium and other minerals. These weak bones can easily fracture during a fall, and can even break during normal activities. The spine, hip and wrist are the most common sites for fracture. Unfortunately, the progress of this disease is often silent, and the first symptoms are fracture and disability.

The good news is that osteoporosis can be prevented and treated. Prevention is best begun in childhood, because the amount of bone—what doctors call "peak bone mass"—achieved before the age of 35 is an important predictor of risk. The key to prevention is building healthy bones through good nutrition (especially adequate amounts of calcium and vitamin D), regular physical activity, a healthy lifestyle and medical therapy when appropriate. It's never too late to start!

RISK FACTORS FOR OSTEOPOROSIS

There are many risk factors for osteoporosis. Check off any risk factors that may apply to you.

- ❏ I am a Caucasian or Asian woman.
- ❏ I am underweight or small boned.
- ❏ There is a history of osteoporosis in my family.
- ❏ I am postmenopausal. (The rate of bone loss increases rapidly after menopause, whether natural or surgical. The body's estrogen helps women maintain and build healthy bones.)
- ❏ I have used a corticosteroid medication such as prednisone for a long time.
- ❏ I am at least 50 and have a personal history of fractures.

TIPS FOR PREVENTION

- Hormone replacement therapy (HRT) can slow bone loss after menopause. Talk to your doctor to find out if hormones are right for you.

- Regular weight-bearing physical activity throughout life builds healthy bones. How active are you?

- Smoking promotes bone loss. If you smoke, quit!

- Calcium and other vitamins and minerals are essential for good bone health. How's your calcium intake?

▣ Diets high in protein, sodium and caffeine have little effect on bone health. Unfortunately, soft drinks, tea and coffee often replace good sources of calcium, such as nonfat milk and fortified orange juice.

▣ Eating disorders such as bulimia and anorexia nervosa are associated with poor bone health and osteoporosis.

CALCIUM TO THE RESCUE!

Calcium is essential for bone health, but it also has several other important roles in the body, such as nerve function, muscle contraction and blood clotting. The body contains more calcium than any other mineral. Most of your calcium—99 percent of it—is stored in your bones. If you don't get enough calcium from your diet, your body steals it from your bones and teeth. Milk, yogurt and cheese supply 75 percent of dietary calcium. A high intake of dietary calcium may also prevent high blood pressure and colon cancer.

Although it's easy to get all the calcium you need from a healthy eating plan, the majority of women only get about half of the calcium they need for bone health. According to the National Academy of Sciences, adults ages 19 to 50 should get around 1,000 milligrams of calcium each day. Those ages 50 or over should aim for 1,200 milligrams. If your risk for osteoporosis is high, some experts recommend 1,500 milligrams. Check out the following high-calcium eating plan:

Three servings of low-fat dairy (a serving is 8 ounces of milk or yogurt)	~ 900 to 1,000 mg
1 to 1.5 ounces of cheese (a single sandwich slice or a cube the size of your thumb)	~ 200 mg
8 ounces of calcium-fortified orange juice	~ 300 mg
Healthful diet (dark green leafy vegetables, fruits, whole grains and legumes)	~ 200 to 400 mg
TOTAL	~ 1,600 to 1,900 mg

If you're lactose intolerant or a strict vegan (no dairy), it can be more difficult to meet your daily calcium needs. Many people who are lactose intolerant can drink smaller servings of milk—start with 2- to 4-ounce servings—or drink it with meals. Yogurt, cheese and buttermilk are often easier to digest. Try using a reduced lactose milk or lactase enzyme. Other good sources of calcium include tofu processed with calcium and calcium-fortified foods such as orange juice, soy milk and cereals. Also eat lots of dark green leafy vegetables, fruits, whole grains, legumes and nuts.

WHAT ABOUT CALCIUM SUPPLEMENTS?

Food sources are your first choice because they contain other important nutrients your body needs and are best absorbed by your body. However, if your diet falls short, a supplement such as calcium carbonate or calcium citrate may be a good idea. Talk to your doctor about what's best for you.

If you choose to supplement, only supplement the amount of calcium you need—small doses of 500 milligrams *elemental calcium* or less are best. Elemental calcium refers to the amount of calcium in a supplement that's available for your body to absorb. Most calcium supplements list the amount of elemental calcium on the label. However, some brands list only the total weight of each tablet in milligrams. This is the weight of the calcium, plus whatever it's bound to—such as carbonate, citrate, lactate or gluconate.

The simplest way to determine how much elemental calcium is in a supplement is to look at the Nutrition Facts label. For calcium, the Percent Daily Value (% DV) is based on 1,000 mg of elemental calcium, so every 10 percent in the Daily Value column represents 100 mg of elemental calcium (0.10 x 1,000 mg = 100 mg). For example, if a calcium supplement has 60 percent of the Daily Value, it contains 600 mg of elemental calcium (0.60 x 1,000 mg = 600 mg). When choosing a calcium supplement, you should also:

- **Note the serving size.** This will tell you the number of tablets you need to get the %DV listed on the label.

▨ **Check the label for the abbreviation "USP."** The best supplements meet the voluntary standards of the U.S. Pharmacopeia (USP) for quality, purity and tablet disintegration or dissolution.

▨ **Avoid calcium supplements that contain unrefined oyster shell, bone meal or dolomite.** These products may also contain toxic substances such as lead, mercury and arsenic.

▨ **Don't bother with chelated calcium tablets.** They're more expensive and have no advantage over other types of calcium.

It's best to take a calcium supplement with a meal to help absorption, but not with a meal high in calcium-rich foods. Your body can only absorb so much calcium at a time.

THE ROLE OF PHYSICAL ACTIVITY

Studies show that active men and women have healthier bones. The bones adapt to the stress of regular weight-bearing physical activity by becoming stronger. Good activities include walking, jogging, aerobics, strength training and recreational sports that keep you on your feet. Recent studies show that strength training can slow down and even reverse the loss of bone that occurs in postmenopausal women. Doing some activity in the sunshine a few days a week can give you an additional boost—more vitamin D!

A WORD ABOUT VITAMIN D

Vitamin D helps your body use calcium to build healthy bones. If you drink milk, you're likely getting enough vitamin D. Your skin can also produce vitamin D with the help of sunshine; 10 to 15 minutes a few days each week is all you

GOING, GOING, GONE

Women can lose up to 20 percent of their bone mass in the five to seven years following menopause, making them more likely to develop osteoporosis.[2]

need. If you don't drink milk or you get little sunshine, you may need to consider a supplement—400 international units (IUs) up to 2,000 IUs per day.

GOOD CALCIUM SOURCES

FOOD	AMOUNT	CALCIUM (mg.)
Yogurt, plain, low-fat	8 oz.	415
Collards, frozen, boiled	1 cup	357
Skim milk	1 cup	306
Spinach, frozen, boiled	1 cup	291
Black-eyed peas, boiled	1 cup	211
Canned salmon	3 oz.	181
Baked beans, canned	1 cup	154
Cottage cheese, 1% milkfat	1 cup	138

Notes

1. "Fast Facts," National Osteoporosis Foundation. http://www.nof.org/osteoporosis/disease facts.htm (accessed October 2007).
2. Ibid.

understanding high blood pressure

High blood pressure is a silent killer. According to the National Heart, Lung, and Blood Institute, about 65 million Americans (nearly one in three)—and more than half of all Americans 60 and older—have high blood pressure.[1] As many as 21 million don't even know they have high blood pressure because it usually causes no symptoms.[2] The fact is, if your blood pressure is high, you're at a much greater risk for heart attack, stroke and kidney disease. It's important to know your blood pressure and take steps to bring it down if it's high. A healthy lifestyle can lower your risk of developing high blood pressure in the future.

WHAT IS BLOOD PRESSURE?

You've probably had your blood pressure measured before, but you may not know what the two numbers mean. The numbers tell you how hard your blood is pressing on the walls of your arteries as it flows through your body. If your blood pressure is high, your heart and arteries are working too hard and this can result in damage to the heart, arteries and organs such as the brain and kidneys.

The first or top number is the *systolic pressure*. This is the pressure created in the arteries when the heart contracts. The second or bottom number is the *diastolic pressure*. This refers to the pressure in the arteries when the heart relaxes between beats. What are your blood-pressure numbers?

RISK CLASSIFICATION CHART

	SYSTOLIC (MMHG)	DIASTOLIC (MMHG)	MY BLOOD PRESSURE
Normal	Less than 120	Less than 80	
Prehypertension	120 to 139	80 to 89	
Stage 1 Hypertension	140 to 159	90 to 99	
Stage 2 Hypertension	160 or higher	100 or higher	

CAUSES OF HIGH BLOOD PRESSURE

Doctors don't know all the factors that cause high blood pressure. In at least 90 percent of people, in fact, the cause is unknown. In such cases, the diagnosis is called "primary" or "essential" hypertension. High blood pressure often runs in families and the risk increases with age. If you have prehypertension, you're also at greater risk for high blood pressure (see risk classification chart, above). Several lifestyle factors also seem to be associated with high blood pressure: weight gain and obesity, a sedentary lifestyle and poor dietary habits.

PREVENTION OF HIGH BLOOD PRESSURE

The National Heart, Lung, and Blood Institute suggests taking the following eight steps to help prevent and control blood pressure.[3]

1 Talk with your physician. Find out what your blood pressure numbers are and what they mean.

2 Take medicine as prescribed. Listen to your doctor rather than try to treat it yourself.

3 Achieve and maintain a healthy weight. As your body weight rises, blood pressure often rises too. If you are overweight, losing as little as 10 percent of your weight can significantly decrease your risk of developing high blood pressure, or lower it if it's high. Monitor your blood pressure every few months as you lose weight.

4 Follow a healthy eating plan. The National High Blood Pressure Education Program recommends adequate intake of potassium and a diet rich in fruits, vegetables, low-fat dairy products, and reduced saturated and total fat. A study called DASH—Dietary Approaches to Stop Hypertension—found that eating certain foods can lower blood pressure as effectively as taking medication.[4] DASH researchers don't understand all the reasons that this eating plan is so beneficial. One reason may be its high potassium, magnesium and calcium content.

5 Reduce salt and sodium intake. Studies have shown that limiting sodium to less than 2,300 mg (about 1 teaspoon of salt) per day can help lower or control blood pressure. It is important to read labels.

6 Get and stay physically active. Regular moderate physical activity can lower your blood pressure and improve your health and well-being. Try to do at least 30 minutes of activity on most, preferably all, days of the week. Select an activity that requires some exertion but is comfortable and enjoyable. Continue this activity on a regular basis; when it becomes less challenging,

THE DASH DIET

- High in fruits and vegetables (4 to 5 servings of each daily)
- High in low-fat dairy foods (2 to 3 servings daily)
- High in grains such as breads, cereal, rice and pasta (6 or more servings daily)
- Lean meat, chicken or fish daily (no more than six 1-ounce servings daily)
- Legumes, nuts and seeds (4 to 5 servings weekly, with more beans than nuts or seeds)
- Low in fat and saturated fat (no more than 2 to 3 daily servings of fats such as oils, margarine, mayonnaise or salad dressing)
- Low in sweets (no more than 5 low-fat sweets each week—fruit is the preferred dessert)

gradually increase the time or intensity or add another activity you enjoy.

7 Limit alcohol consumption. In addition to increasing blood pressure, excessive alcohol consumption can cause a variety of other serious health problems, such as liver, kidney or heart disease. As a general rule, men should drink no more than two drinks a day; women, a maximum of one.

8 Quit smoking. It increases your risk of developing a stroke, heart disease, peripheral arterial disease and several forms of cancer.

WARNING SIGNS

About 45 million Americans have prehypertension, which puts them at twice the risk of developing high blood pressure later in life, according to the National Heart, Lung, and Blood Institute.[5]

Notes

1. "Landmark Hypertension Treatment Study Launches Extensive Physician and Patient Education Program to Improve Public Health," National Heart, Lung and Blood Institute, February 1, 2006. http://www.nhlbi.nih.gov/new/press/06-02-01.htm (accessed October 2007).
2. "High Blood Pressure and Chronic Kidney Disease (Stages 1-4)," National Kidney Foundation, 2004. http://www.kidney.org/atoz/pdf/hbpandckd.pdf (accessed October 2007).
3. "Your Guide to Lowering Blood Pressure," U.S. Department of Health and Human Services, May 2003. http://www.nhlbi.nih.gov/health/public/heart/hbp/hbp_low/hbp_low.pdf (accessed November 2007).
4. For more information, visit http://www.nhlbi.nih.gov/health/public/heart/hbp/dash/new_dash.pdf.
5. "The Seventh Report of the Joint National Committee on Prevention, Detection, Evaluation and Treatment of High Blood Pressure," *Hypertension*, 2003 (42):1206.

adding flavor the healthy way!

LOWERING SALT INTAKE

When it comes to cardiovascular health, sodium (salt) has drawn a considerable amount of attention because of its relationship to high blood pressure. High blood pressure is a leading risk factor for heart attack, stroke and kidney disease. Scientists have discovered that some people's blood pressure is very sensitive to excess sodium in the diet.

Because high blood pressure is such a serious health problem, the current U.S. Dietary Guidelines call for Americans to choose a diet moderate in salt and sodium. According to the American Heart Association, more than 75 percent of salt in the American diet comes from processed foods, not the saltshaker. Only about 15 percent of the sodium in the average diet is added in the kitchen or at the table.[1] The top sources of salt in the diet include processed meats, prepackaged meals, fast foods, canned and dry soups, cheese, salted snack foods and certain condiments.

The best way to learn how much sodium is in a food is to read the label. Foods that provide more than 300 milligrams per serving are particularly high in sodium. For a single food item to carry the term "healthy" on the label, it must contain 360 or fewer milligrams of sodium per serving. Here are some foods particularly high in sodium.

- Regular canned and dry soups—1 cup contains 600 to 1,300 mg
- Some prepackaged meals (e.g., frozen dinners)—8 ounces contain 500 to 1,570 mg
- Regular soy sauce—1 tablespoon contains 1,030 mg
- Salted popcorn—2 $1/2$ cups contain 330 mg
- Processed cheese and cheese spreads—1 ounce contains 340 to 450 mg
- Cured ham—3 ounces contain 1,025 mg

While we're born with a preference for sweet tastes, salt is an acquired taste. Many people find that after cutting down on salt, many foods that they used to enjoy taste too salty. Cut down gradually to give your taste buds time to adapt. To be sure you consume no more than 2,300 mg of sodium (the equivalent of 1 teaspoon of salt) per day, try these helpful tips.

- Choose foods that are naturally low in sodium, such as fresh fruits and vegetables.
- Break the habit of adding salt during cooking—there's no reason to salt cooking water—or at the table.
- Rinse canned meats, legumes and vegetables under cold water to remove excess salt.
- Eat a variety of foods during a single meal to stimulate the taste buds.
- Eat meals slowly and savor the flavor and aroma of each bite.
- Cut the salt called for in most recipes by half (or more).
- For meals with dried seasoning packets, use half or less of the packet to cut down on the sodium.
- Learn to season foods with herbs, spices, fruit juice and flavored vinegars.
- Limit processed meats such as ham, bacon, hot dogs and lunch meats.
- Limit high-salt condiments such as soy sauce, steak sauce, barbecue sauce, mustard and ketchup.
- Buy reduced-salt or low-salt snack foods.

- Limit consumption of olives, pickles, relishes and many salad dressings that are loaded with salt.
- When eating out, ask for meals to be prepared with less salt, ask for sauces to be served on the side and avoid using the saltshaker.

HERBS AND SPICES

Adding herbs, spices or other flavorings is a great way to make tasty dishes that are low in sodium. You'll have to experiment to find out what works best for you. Here are some tips on using and storing herbs and spices.

- Read the label—some premixed spices contain salt.
- Store herbs and spices in a cool, dark place and in tight containers. Avoid heat, moisture and light.
- Date dry herbs and spices when you buy them—shelf life is about one year.
- Test the freshness of herbs by rubbing them between your fingers and checking the aroma.
- Crumbling dry herbs between your fingers before using releases more flavor.
- Liquid brings out the flavor of dried herbs and spices.
- If you use fresh herbs, store them in a plastic bag in the refrigerator. Before using, wash and pat dry.
- For soups and stews (dishes that cook awhile), add herbs and spices toward the end of cooking.
- For chilled dishes or meats, the earlier you add the herbs and spices, the better the flavor.
- When trying new herbs and spices, add them gradually to the dish—you can always add more.

REDUCE YOUR RISK OF HIGH BLOOD PRESSURE

Clinical studies have shown that reducing salt intake lowers blood pressure in people with and without high blood pressure. In 2006, the American Heart Association advised Americans to reduce salt intake to about 1.5 grams (1,500 mg) a day and asked food manufacturers to reduce salts in food by 50 percent. By taking action, you reduce your risk of developing hypertension.

SEASONING IDEAS FOR MEAT AND VEGETABLES

Beef	Bay leaf, dry mustard, marjoram, nutmeg, onion, pepper, sage, thyme
Fish	Curry powder, dill, dry mustard, lemon juice, marjoram, paprika, pepper
Poultry	Ginger, marjoram, oregano, paprika, rosemary, sage, tarragon, thyme
Carrots	Cinnamon, cloves, marjoram, nutmeg, rosemary, sage
Corn	Cumin, curry powder, green pepper, onion, paprika, parsley
Green beans	Dill, curry powder, lemon juice, marjoram, oregano, tarragon, thyme
Peas	Basil, dill, ginger, marjoram, onion, parsley, sage
Potatoes	Basil, dill, garlic, onion, paprika, parsley, rosemary, sage
Squash	Allspice, basil, cinnamon, curry powder, ginger, marjoram, nutmeg, onion, rosemary, sage
Tomatoes	Basil, bay leaf, dill, marjoram, onion, oregano, parsley, pepper, thyme

Note

1. "Shake Your Salt Habit," American Heart Association, July 25, 2007. http://www.heart.org/pre senter.jhtml?identifier=2106 (accessed November 2007).

convenience foods—
making the most of your time

Our fast-paced lives sometimes require us to cook and eat on the run. Grocery store aisles are filled with convenience foods of all types—frozen dinners, canned soups, ready-to-eat cereals—and they come in all types of packages—jars, cans, bottles, boxes and bags. These foods save us time, but they can also be high in calories, fat, cholesterol, added sugars and sodium. Don't let busyness become a roadblock to achieving and maintaining a healthy weight and following a nutritious eating plan. Even in the area of convenience foods, the keys to healthy nutrition are balance, moderation and variety.

WATCH OUT FOR TRENDS

In the 1990s, the most popular trend in convenience foods was the introduction of *low-fat* foods. Low-fat versions of our favorite foods were everywhere. You would think with all the low-fat foods available, Americans would be skinnier than ever. But people tended to eat more, and many actually gained weight on low-fat or no-fat ice cream, cookies, yogurt, and so forth. The problem: *Low fat doesn't necessarily mean low calorie!*

PRODUCT	CALORIES	PRODUCT	CALORIES
Chocolate cream-filled cookie	53	Fat-free version	55
Fig bar	60	Fat-free version	70
Granola cereal	130	Reduced-fat version	110
Breakfast bar	120	Reduced-fat version	120
3-ounce bagel	150	Today's bigger version	400

Then the pendulum swung to low-carb foods. Suddenly, steaks and butter were all the rage while carbs became taboo. The Atkins Diet instructed millions of Americans how to lose weight by eating more fat and cholesterol. A lot of restaurants added Atkins-friendly menu items, and manufacturers jumped on the bandwagon by unveiling low-carb, high-fat offerings.

Low-carb diets hit their peak by 2005, though some manufacturers still offer low-carb choices. The fact is, low-carb diets don't work long-term. The majority of successful dieters who are part of the National Weight Control Registry follow a diet low in fat and high in fiber-rich carbs such as fruits and vegetables. Only 1 percent of them follow a high-protein, high-fat diet.[1]

CHOOSING HEALTHY CONVENIENCE FOODS

Dinners and single-item foods can fit into your daily balance of calories, fat, cholesterol, sodium, fiber and sugar. Use the following guidelines to help you choose healthier convenience foods.

LOOK FOR FOODS	LOOK FOR CLUES ON THE FOOD LABEL	KNOW YOUR DAILY GOAL
Low in fat	3 or fewer grams of fat per serving	30 percent or less of total calories
Low in saturated fat	1 gram or less of saturated fat per serving	7 to 10 percent of total calories
Low in cholesterol	60 or fewer milligrams of cholesterol per serving	300 or fewer milligrams

LOOK FOR FOODS	LOOK FOR CLUES ON THE FOOD LABEL	KNOW YOUR DAILY GOAL
Low in sodium	400 or fewer milligrams of sodium per serving	2,300 or fewer milligrams
High in fiber	2.5 or more grams of fiber per serving	14 grams per 1,000 calories consumed
High in nutrients	10 percent or more of the DRI for one or more of the following: vitamin A, vitamin C, iron, calcium, protein and fiber	100 percent of the DRI

When choosing frozen dinners or entrées, use the following guidelines:

- Choose dinners that have fewer than 400 calories, 15 grams of fat, 5 grams of saturated fat and 800 mg of sodium.

- Choose entrées with fewer than 300 calories, 10 grams of fat and 4 grams of saturated fat.

USING CONVENIENCE FOODS

- Compare food labels when shopping for convenience foods. Choose the food with the lowest saturated fat, cholesterol and sodium.

- When cooking packaged foods such as instant noodles or macaroni and cheese, lower the fat and calories by using less butter or margarine than the directions call for. Use half of the seasoning packet, or use your own seasonings, to lower the sodium content. Add your own fresh or frozen vegetables to add fiber, vitamins and minerals.

- When buying canned meat such as chicken, tuna or salmon, choose water-packed varieties instead of oil-packed.

- Choose breakfast cereals with terms such as "high fiber," "whole grain" or "bran" on the label. Cereals that are high in fiber (>2.5 grams per serving) and low in added sugar are good choices.

THE ORGANIC BOOM

In 2005, the U.S. organic industry grew 17 percent overall to reach $14.6 billion in consumer sales. Specifically, organic foods—the largest and most clearly defined part of the organic industry—grew 16.2 percent in 2005 and accounted for $13.8 billion in consumer sales.[2]

As organic foods become part of the American mainstream, supermarkets that offer organic foods are popping up all across the nation. But are organic foods really any healthier than conventionally grown foods? The jury is still out. According to professional organizations and government agencies like the American Dietetic Association and the USDA, there is a lack of strong evidence that organics are safer or healthier. At this point in time, the choice between buying organic or conventionally grown food is truly a personal preference.

Food safety experts say that organic or not, consumers should observe the same rules regarding food safety. Thoroughly wash—even scrub—all produce. And, if the skin won't come clean, peel it off.

Store potentially hazardous foods at appropriate temperatures to prevent food-borne illness (this includes meat, poultry, shellfish, cooked rice or beans, baked or broiled potatoes, sprouts, tofu, garlic and oil mixtures, melon and milk products).

- Canned or frozen fruits and vegetables are good choices, but watch out for sodium and added fats. Rinse vegetables, beans and canned meats with water to reduce the sodium content. Avoid canned and frozen vegetables with high-fat sauces.

- Limit use of frozen dinners and entrées with breaded or fried meats and vegetables.

- Buy prepackaged salads that contain an assortment of lettuce and other fresh vegetables. Be wary of salads that come with their own dressings and croutons, which are high in fat.

- Increase nutrients by balancing out your meal with a piece of fruit and a low-fat dairy product such as skim milk.

- Prepare your own healthy convenience foods by cooking your own recipes and freezing the leftovers in individual servings. Freezer bags and a variety of plastic containers make it convenient for you to store and reheat your meals.

Notes

1. S. M. Shick, R. R. Wing, M. L. Klem, et al, "Persons Successful at Long-term Weight Loss and Maintenance Continue to Consume a Low Calorie, Low Fat Diet," *Journal of the American Dietetic Association*, 1998, (98):408-413.

2. "U.S. Organic Industry Review," Organic Trade Association, 2006. http://www.ota.com/pics/doc uments/short%20overview%20MMS.pdf (accessed November 2007).

dining
on the go!

Years ago, dining out was usually reserved for special occasions and celebrations. Today, Americans eat out regularly. Fast-food drive-thrus and restaurants offer convenience when we're running errands, taking a break during the workday or traveling on business. People who are calorie-conscious or want healthy meals are presented with mind-boggling choices and temptations. The following suggestions and charts are designed with you in mind. They will help you make informed decisions as you select from diverse menus and cuisines. *Bon appétit!*

BEST BETS FOR A HEALTHY LUNCH

A fast-food meal can easily top 1,000 calories and give you a day's worth of fat, cholesterol and sodium—but you *can* make healthy fast-food choices during your lunch hour.

Today, most fast-food restaurants offer a variety of healthier foods such as grilled chicken, salads, baked potatoes and deli-style sandwiches. Unfortunately, fresh fruits and vegetables are hard to find. The key is to plan ahead and be prepared to make healthy choices. Look for ways to trim fat, cut calories and add variety whenever you can. Consider the following suggestions.

■ A fresh salad with an assortment of colorful vegetables, low-fat dressing *(On the side, please!)*, grilled chicken, grilled chicken sandwich *(Hold the mayo!)*, bean and cheese burrito *(Go easy on the cheese and add extra lettuce and tomato!)*, small hamburger or baked potato *(Toppings on the side!)* are all good choices. All these meals have fewer than 400 calories and 30 percent or less fat.

■ Deli sandwiches don't have to be off-limits. Choose lean meats such as turkey, ham or roast beef. Ask for mustard or light mayonnaise. Request less meat (usually half the typical serving), more lettuce, tomato and other vegetables, and whole-grain bread. Hold the chips or fries.

■ Even pizza can be a healthy selection. If possible, stick to veggie pizza, and ask for less cheese and more sauce and vegetables. Limit yourself to one or two slices of thin-crust pizza. Eat a salad, too, with low-fat dressing on the side.

EAST MEETS WEST

With the diversity of Asian cuisine—Chinese, Japanese, Thai, Indian, Korean and Vietnamese—and cooking styles, it's important to know how to read menus. The following chart of the most common menu items and terms will aid you in choosing wisely.

LOW IN FAT	HIGH IN FAT	HIGH IN SODIUM
Barbecued	Coconut milk	Black bean sauce
Bean curd	Duck	Hoisin sauce
Braised	Egg rolls	Miso sauce
Roasted or grilled	Fried or crispy	Most soups
Simmered	Fried rice or noodles	Oyster sauce
Steamed	Peanuts or cashews	Pickled
Stir-fried	Tempura	Soy sauce
Water chestnuts	Wonton	Teriyaki sauce

Keep the following tips in mind:

- Some Asian sauces, such as sweet-and-sour and plum sauce, are actually low in fat, calories and sodium. The problem is that dishes served with these sauces often consist of deep-fried meats.

- A tablespoon of soy sauce has nearly 1,000 mg of sodium—almost half of the recommended daily intake of 2,300 mg.

- Japanese sushi—a combination of raw fish, vinegared rice and (often) seaweed—is actually low in fat, calories and sodium, depending on the dipping sauce.

SOUTH OF THE BORDER

It's easy to consume 500 calories or more at a Mexican restaurant before your meal even arrives! Plan ahead to limit the number of chips you eat (five to eight chips equal 100 calories). Better yet, ask that chips not be brought to your table. Order steamed corn tortillas instead.

To make healthy choices, become familiar with a few Spanish terms and cooking methods. Then go for the healthier, low-fat items.

LOW IN FAT	HIGH IN FAT
Baked, broiled, simmered or *asada* (grilled)	*Chili con queso* (cheese sauce)
Fajitas (grilled meat and soft tortillas)	*Chorizo* (sausage)
Picante sauce or salsa	Fried or crispy
Salsa verde (green sauce)	Guacamole and sour cream
Veracruz or *ranchero* (tomato-based) sauces	Refried, often with lard

Thoughts to consider before you order:

- Tortilla or bean soup and a salad are a healthy start to your meal—they can even be the whole meal! Ask for the salad dressing, guacamole and sour cream to be served on the side. Salsa makes a nutritious no-fat dressing. If your salad is served in a tortilla shell, remove it and concentrate on the veggies.

- Mexican dinners tend to be large. Avoid combination or deluxe plates, and order à la carte or side orders instead. Another option is to split a combination plate with a companion.

- Fajitas with grilled chicken or lean meat are a good option. Instead of cheese, guacamole and sour cream, ask for extra lettuce, tomatoes and salsa instead.

A TASTE OF ITALY

You may not speak Italian, but you can learn how to read the menu. Learn the following common terms to help you make more healthful choices.

LOW IN FAT	HIGH IN FAT
Baked, broiled or roasted	*Alfredo*—butter or cheese sauce
Marsala (wine sauce) or *cacciatore* (with stewed vegetables)	Cheese- or meat-filled pastas (such as ravioli, manicotti or cannelloni)
Marinara—tomato-based sauce	*Crema*—cream-based sauce
Minestrone	*Fritto*—fried
Primavera—with fresh vegetables	Garlic bread
Red or white clam sauce	*Parmigiana*—breaded and deep-fried meat

Some friendly guidelines:

- Just because it's green doesn't mean it's low-fat! *Pesto*, made with basil, olive oil, pine nuts and grated cheese, is generally high in fat and calories. Use it judiciously!

- When ordering pizza, choose a thin crust and ask for less cheese (or even no cheese). Select vegetables as toppings instead of high-fat and high-sodium meats.

- Ask if the restaurant serves whole-grain pasta. In all likelihood, it may not be an option—but if enough consumers start requesting it, the restaurant may add whole-grain pasta to the menu.

BREAKFAST IN THE FAST LANE

Breakfast may be the most important meal of the day. Studies show that regular breakfast eaters consume more nutrients throughout the day, which means that regular breakfast eaters are more likely to get adequate levels of minerals such as calcium, phosphorus and magnesium, and vitamins such as riboflavin, folate and vitamins A, C and B_{12}.

Try to eat a balanced breakfast high in complex carbohydrates, some protein and a little fat. It will stay with you longer and give you the energy you need to make it through the morning.

FOOD CLUES

Menus are full of food clues if you know what to look for. Here is a list of terms often used in menus that will help you order wisely.

Less Fat	More Fat
Baked or broiled	Fried
Poached	Breaded
Grilled	Sautéed (in butter or oil)
Tomato sauce	Alfredo or cream sauce
Roasted	Casserole
Steamed	Prime

If you find yourself eating breakfast away from home or in the car, the following tips will help you make healthy choices:

- Hot and cold cereals are a good choice at any restaurant.

- Pancakes and waffles can be an acceptable choice if you go easy on the butter or margarine. Top them with fresh fruit, jam, jelly or syrup.

- Order fruit juice and low-fat milk instead of coffee or a soft drink.

- Eggs are a good choice because they are a good source of protein, iron and vitamin A. It's the egg yolks that are high in cholesterol; ask for scrambled eggs without the yolk or made with an egg substitute.

- A bagel or English muffin can be a good choice, but watch the butter and cream cheese. If the bagel is large, cut it in half—and enjoy it with a piece of fruit.

WATCH FOR HIDDEN FATS

When eating away from home, it can be difficult to estimate how much fat is in a meal. It's important to estimate hidden fats in food because extra calories can add up quickly. Just one teaspoon of oil or one tablespoon of salad dressing has 5 grams of fat and 45 calories. Considering that a ladle of dressing at most salad bars is three or four tablespoons, it's easy to see how fat calories can add up!

The best way to control hidden fats when eating out is to ask that foods be prepared without added fats and that salad dressing, gravies and sauces be served on the side.

the amazing 10-minute workout!

No time, *no fun* and *bo-o-o-ring!* These are common reasons people give for not making physical activity a lifetime habit. Yet experts are making it harder and harder to come up with good excuses. The latest recommendations tell us that exercise doesn't have to be hard to be beneficial. Gone are the days when you had to exercise for at least 30 minutes at a certain heart rate to get the health and fitness benefits of aerobic exercise. What's the exercise prescription for today? *Something is better than nothing, and more is better than something.*

The latest recommendations from groups such as the American Heart Association and the American College of Sports Medicine call for at least 30 minutes of moderate physical activity on as many days of the week as possible—preferably every day. The latest twist on this new recommendation is that the activity doesn't have to be done all at one time. Shorter amounts accumulated over the course of a day appear to offer the same health benefits as the more traditional 30 continuous minutes of exercise.

THE BENEFITS OF SHORTER WORKOUTS

Shorter workouts are easier to start and easier to stick with. It's easy to get burned out on exercise by doing too much too soon. Start slow and work your way up to longer sessions as your physical activity becomes a habit.

You may also be a person who just doesn't have 30 to 60 minutes to give at one time. Shorter workouts are easier to fit into your schedule and will help fight boredom by allowing more variety in your routine. They're also great for regular exercisers who occasionally miss or are unable to do their usual routine. When you miss a session or know that you are going to miss a session, just slip in one or two of these shorter workouts wherever and whenever you can.

HOW TO DO IT

Are lack of time, lack of enjoyment and boredom among the reasons you have a hard time making exercise a part of your life? Whether you're a regular exerciser or just getting started, consider some of the following ideas for fitting 10-minute workouts into your day:

- Walking can be done anywhere, anytime. Think about times in your typical day when you can fit in a short, brisk walk.
- Get up 10 minutes earlier and fit in a quick walk before starting your day.
- Walk as part of your daily quiet time.
- Take 10-minute walking breaks at work.
- Arrive to work 10 minutes early and walk or climb the stairs.
- Take a 10-minute walk around the mall before stopping to shop.
- Walk your dog for 10 minutes.
- Take the entire family out for a 10-minute walk before or after meals.

SHORT BOUTS PAY OFF

Shorter amounts of activity accumulated over the course of a day appear to offer the same health benefits as the more traditional 30 continuous minutes of exercise. If you don't have time for a 30-minute workout, aim for three 10-minute walks throughout your day.

- Walk around the house during commercials or between shows—you'll easily get in 10 minutes.

Walking is not your only choice. Here are some other ideas.

- Pick up the pace when you're doing household chores—10 minutes of vacuuming, washing the car or working in the yard add up over the course of a day. To get the benefit, however, you have to push the pace a bit. Turn on your favorite music to help keep you moving.
- Buy an exercise video and pop it in for 10 minutes.
- Do you have exercise equipment that's collecting dust? Pull it out and try a 10-minute routine instead of feeling like you have to stay on for 30 minutes or longer.
- Rather than just watching your kids play, spend 10 minutes playing with them—shoot baskets, throw a ball or Frisbee, kick a soccer ball.
- Take 10-minute breaks at work and do calisthenics, strength training or stretching exercises.

Choose a few activities that you enjoy and can do for approximately 10 minutes at a time. Be creative—don't limit yourself to the traditional exercises. Whatever you choose to do, try to make it fun. Remember, the E in "exercise" is for *enjoyment!*

Once you've chosen a few activities, think of times when you can fit them into your day. Think about moments when you can be more active, such as when you watch television, shop, work around the house or take a break.

testing your
health-related fitness

Assessing your health-related fitness levels can give you a road-map of where you are and where you need to be. It's important that you move toward a level of fitness that allows you to be healthy and accomplish your goals in life.

Testing your health-related fitness helps you to:

- Develop and maintain an activity program that's right for you.
- Decide where you need the most work.
- Monitor your progress.
- Get back on track if you notice yourself slipping in a few areas.

THE COMPONENTS OF HEALTH-RELATED FITNESS

When assessing your fitness, four components play an important role in your overall health and fitness. A balanced fitness plan considers each of these areas:

- cardiovascular endurance (aerobic fitness)
- muscular strength and endurance
- flexibility
- body composition

The health-related fitness standards for each of these assessments serve as guidelines. Use the standards to get a basic understanding of your health-related fitness. Regardless of your scores, you can use these assessments to help you monitor your progress. If you fall below the standards listed for one or more of the fitness components, you may need to do some work in those areas. What's most important is that you're participating in a variety of enjoyable and beneficial physical activities.

THE HEALTH-RELATED FITNESS TESTS

Note: While these tests should not pose any special risk for most people, it's important to take a few precautions. If you have any underlying medical problems such as heart disease or arthritis, talk to your doctor before taking any of these assessments. Don't push yourself to your maximum limit on any of these tests. The idea is to learn what you can do comfortably and then use the results to monitor your progress.

Some friendly advice:

- Wear comfortable clothing and shoes appropriate for brisk walking.
- Avoid taking the tests on days when it's extremely hot, cold or windy.
- Have a friend or family member help you administer the tests.
- Before performing any tests, warm up for five minutes with light activity and stretching. Cool down when you have finished.
- If you experience any pain or discomfort during any part of the assessments, stop immediately and consult your physician.

1. How Physically Active Are You?

It's much more important to keep track of your physical activity than it is to know your fitness level. As you increase your physical activity, your health and fitness will improve. Regular aerobic activity is associated with several important benefits, such as a lowered risk for heart disease, improved mood and maintenance of a healthy weight.

> I exercise at least three days each week for 30 minutes at a time doing vigorous activities such as walking briskly, jogging, bicycling, aerobic dance or aerobic sports such as soccer, tennis or basketball. (Circle one.)
>
> *True*   *False*

> I am physically active for at least 30 minutes on most days of the week, doing moderate-intensity activities throughout the day such as brisk walking, yard work, leisurely bicycling, swimming, taking the stairs, playing with the kids or gardening. (Circle one.)
>
> *True*   *False*

Recommendations: Try to meet one or both of these physical activity standards. They represent the level of physical activity necessary for good health. If you're not yet meeting at least one of these standards, plan to get started as soon as you can. However, start slowly and gradually work your way up. Start with 5 or 10 minutes doing an activity that you enjoy. If you're meeting the above standards, you're already doing more than most people. Keep up the good work! Working up to three to five hours of moderate to vigorous activity each week will give you additional fitness benefits and help you achieve and maintain a healthy weight.

2. How Aerobically Fit Are You?

Cardiovascular endurance is important to overall health and fitness. There are a number of ways to assess your cardiovascular endurance and monitor your progress. One of the easiest and safest ways is to do a one-mile walk test.

What You Need

- A flat surface that allows you to measure off a one-mile distance, such as at a track at a local school, a walking path at a park or at a shopping mall.
- A stopwatch or watch with a seconds indicator to keep track of your time

What to Do

- Practice taking your pulse several times before taking the assessment, then walk a mile as quickly as you can without straining.
- At the end of the mile, record your time in minutes and seconds. Take your pulse for 15 seconds immediately upon stopping.
- Multiply your pulse by 4 to get the number of heartbeats per minute.

Health-Related Fitness Standard: A good time is between 15 and 20 minutes (closer to 15 minutes if you're younger than 50). If you can walk the mile in less than 14 minutes, you're doing great.

Recommendations: If you can walk one mile in at least 15 to 20 minutes and you're meeting the activity standard, keep up the good work. To monitor your progress, repeat the test every 6 to 12 weeks. As your fitness improves you'll be able to cover the distance in less time; if you're monitoring your heart rate, you may also notice a gradual drop. If you meet the aerobic fitness standard but not the activity standard, don't get too confident. The only way to maintain your fitness level and get the health benefits you need is to be active on a regular basis.

3. How Fit Are Your Muscles?

Muscular strength and endurance are important aspects of health and fitness, particularly as we age. As you lose strength, daily activities become more difficult. Healthy muscles allow you to participate in a variety of activities with ease and enjoyment. Unfortunately, muscular fitness declines as we age. The only way to maintain healthy muscles is to exercise them on a regular basis. Take the following two tests to assess your muscular strength and endurance.

CURL-UPS

This assessment tests the strength and endurance of the abdominal (stomach) muscles. Weak stomach muscles contribute to the lower-back pain that affects millions of adults. The best way to strengthen your stomach muscles is to do curl-ups.

What You Need
- A carpeted surface or an exercise mat
- A partner to hold your legs and count your curl-ups
- A stopwatch or watch with a seconds indicator to keep track of your time

What to Do
- Lie on your back with your feet flat on the floor and knees bent at a 90-degree angle.
- Fold your arms across your chest.
- Curl up slowly by lifting your shoulders off the ground. Continue to raise your body until your elbows touch your knees. Don't lift up to a sitting position.
- Exhale during the upward movement and inhale on the way down. Don't hold your breath!
- Do as many curl-ups as you comfortably can without straining. Stop at one minute.

Health-Related Fitness Standard: If you can do 15 to 20 curl-ups, you're doing well. If you can do 30 or more, you're doing great.

PUSH-UPS

Doing push-ups is a good way to assess the strength and endurance of your upper body.

What You Need
- A carpeted surface or an exercise mat
- A partner to count your push-ups and watch your form
- A stopwatch or watch with a seconds indicator to keep track of your time

What to Do
- Lie face down with hands shoulder's-width apart, palms face down and legs extended. Women should cross their ankles and push up with their knees on the ground.
- Keeping your back and legs straight, push yourself up with your arms, shoulders and chest until your arms are straight.
- Lower yourself back down until your chest touches the floor.
- Exhale during the upward movement and inhale on the way down. Don't hold your breath!
- Do as many push-ups as you comfortably can without straining. Stop at one minute.

Health-Related Fitness Standard: If you can do 10 to 15 push-ups, you're doing well. If you can do 25 or more, you're doing great.

Recommendations: Experts recommend doing at least two days of strength training each week. It's best to do at least one set of 8 to 10 exercises that work each of the major muscle groups—shoulders, back, chest, arms and legs. You can do strength-building exercises using your own body weight, elastic exercise bands, hand and ankle weights, dumbbells or machines. Are you doing strength-building activities regularly?

4. How Flexible Are You?
It's important to maintain flexibility. Poor flexibility increases feelings of stiffness, limits mobility and may increase the risk of certain injuries. Take the following test to assess your flexibility.

SIT AND REACH

This assessment tests the flexibility of the backs of your legs (the hamstring muscles), hips and lower back.

What You Need
- A carpeted surface or an exercise mat
- A yardstick and strip of masking tape
- A partner to measure your stretch and watch your form

What to Do
- Place the yardstick on the floor and put a long strip of masking tape across the yardstick at the 15-inch mark.
- Sit on the floor with your legs extended, straddling the yardstick. Your feet should be 10 to 12 inches apart. Place your heels at the 15-inch mark with the 0 mark close to you.
- With one hand on top of the other and fingertips even, slowly lean forward as far as you comfortably can along the yardstick. Exhale as you stretch forward and be sure not to bend your knees. Don't bounce or overstretch.
- Perform the test three times and take your best measurement to the nearest inch.

Health-Related Fitness Standard: A good score is 12 to 18 inches. There's probably no health advantage to being able to stretch beyond these limits.

Recommendations: To increase or maintain your flexibility, perform several stretching activities at least three days each week; do them every day if you can. Never stretch to the point of pain, and avoid bouncing or jerking movements. Hold each stretch for 10 to 20 seconds. Avoid stretches that put pressure on your neck, lower back or knees.

monitoring your exercise intensity

Y ou may have heard that to get the benefits of aerobic exercise, you have to exercise within your heart-rate zone. Perhaps you are monitoring your exercise heart rate already. While it's more important to pay attention to how you feel during an activity, monitoring your heart rate can be a helpful tool. If you want to use your heart rate to monitor your exercise intensity, use the simple formula below to calculate your heart rate zone.

HOW SHOULD PHYSICAL ACTIVITY FEEL?

A beneficial level of physical activity will feel like you're pushing yourself somewhat. The activity should cause some increase in breathing, but you should still be able to carry on a conversation. If you can't keep up the intensity for at least 30 minutes, you're working too hard. You should also feel back to normal within 30 minutes after a workout. You don't have to break into a sweat or feel your muscles burn to get the health and fitness benefits of physical activity.

WHY MONITOR MY EXERCISE HEART RATE?

To deliver oxygen to your muscles during activity, your heart must pump stronger and faster. The harder you work, the faster your heart beats. Because your heart rate reflects the intensity of exercise, you can use it to monitor how hard you're working. Researchers have determined that exercising at 60 to 85 percent of your predicted maximum heart rate results in significant health and fitness benefits.

WHAT IS A PREDICTED MAXIMUM HEART RATE?

Everyone has a maximum heart rate. When your heart reaches its limit, the muscles can't get all the oxygen they need, so your body has to slow down. Fortunately, it's not necessary to work at this maximum level to get the benefits of aerobic exercise. Most people don't know their true maximum heart rate (some fitness centers provide testing); however, you can calculate your predicted maximum heart rate this way:

Subtract your age from 220.

220 – _____ [your age] = _____ [maximum heart rate]

Once you know your predicted maximum heart rate, you can determine your calculated heart-rate zone. To find your zone, multiply your maximum heart rate by 60 percent and 85 percent:

Maximum heart rate _____ x .60 = _____ [lower end of zone]
Maximum heart rate _____ x .85 = _____ [higher end of zone]

COUNTING THE COST

One question almost everyone asks is, *How much physical activity is enough?* One way to answer this question is to count the cost—in calories that is! Scientific evidence reveals that an energy expenditure of 1,000 to 2,000 calories per week (150 to 300 calories per day) provides most of the health benefits associated with physical activity. Use the following chart to see if you're on track.

CALORIES BURNED			
ACTIVITY	PER MINUTE	IN 30 MINUTES	IN ONE HOUR
Brisk walking (15 to 20 minutes per mile)	5	150	300
Gardening (digging, planting, weeding)	5	150	300
Golf (walking)	5	150	300
Housework (mopping, washing windows)	5	150	300
Water aerobics	5	150	300
Leisurely bicycling (10 mph)	6	180	360
Yard work (shoveling, mowing, raking)	6	180	360
Weight training and calisthenics	6	180	360
Hiking	7	210	420
Step aerobics	7	210	420
Tennis (doubles)	7	210	420
In-line skating	8	240	480
Power walking	8	240	480
Stair-climbing machine	8	240	480
Tennis (singles)	8	240	480
Bicycling (12 mph)	9	270	540
Ski machine	9	270	540
Swimming (moderate effort)	9	270	540
Basketball	10	300	600
Jogging (12 minutes per mile)	10	300	600
Walking up stairs	10	300	600
Running (10 minutes per mile)	14	420	840

buying home equipment

T he great thing about home fitness equipment is that it gives you the flexibility to work out anytime, regardless of weather conditions and without leaving the comfort of your own home. The most popular pieces of fitness equipment purchased for home use are *treadmills* and *stationary bikes*.

CONSIDERATIONS BEFORE PURCHASING

1 *Make sure the equipment is comfortable;* otherwise, you won't want to use it. This is the most important factor aside from the price.

2 *Shop wisely.* Check out the manufacturer's rating. Some pieces of equipment, for example, are only built to handle up to 210 pounds.

3 *Make sure the equipment is simple to operate* with a safety button for stopping.

4 *Try it out* and ask for a demonstration of all the features.

5 *Consider the manufacturer's warranty.* Most home exercise equipment carries some type of warranty against defects in workmanship, which can range from 90 days for parts and labor to a lifetime warranty.

6 *Check the classifieds.* You can find nearly new equipment for sale by individuals who are tired of using it for a clothes rack!

OTHER MACHINES TO CONSIDER

- NordicTrack™ ski machines: They're easy on the knees, have an adjustable pace, do not take up much space and are quiet.
- Cardio Glide Plus™ (similar to a HealthRider™) has no impact on the joints. It doesn't put a strain on the knees, gives a gentle full-body workout and has adjustable resistance.
- Elliptical cross trainer: This is a no-impact aerobic device that's a cross between a ski machine, a Stairmaster® and a bicycle (without a seat).

choosing a personal trainer

There are several advantages to hiring a personal trainer to improve your physical workout. Here's what a personal trainer can do:

- **Help you get started if you are new to exercise.** Whether you've joined a health club or exercise at home, a personal trainer can customize a plan for you and help you reach your goals, giving you the confidence to go it alone.

- **Show you new ways to maximize your workout.** Is your routine in a lull? A personal trainer can introduce you to new cardiovascular activities, strength training, flexibility exercises and balance moves, and help you achieve a new level of fitness. You may be more inclined to push yourself if you are working with a trainer.

- **Work with your special needs.** If you have medical problems or physical limitations, don't give up! Personal trainers who have been trained to work with certain medical issues can be a huge asset and encouragement.

- **Develop a program for time-challenged people.** A good workout may take less time than you think. Make the most of your time by hiring someone who can develop a sound program for you.

- **"Coach" you in your weight-loss journey.** Through the encouragement of a personal trainer, you can learn in what areas your exercise program or even your diet might be missing the mark.

FINDING THE BEST TRAINER

1 **It's hard to beat word-of-mouth.** If you have friends who have been satisfied with their personal trainer—and you have noticed significant results firsthand—ask for contact information.

2 **What is the trainer's educational background? Is he or she certified?** In an ideal world, the trainer will have a college degree in physical education, sports medicine, kinesiology or a fitness-related field. Otherwise, the trainer should be certified by a reputable organization such as the American Council on Exercise, the American College of Sports Medicine, The Cooper Institute or the National Strength and Conditioning Association.

3 **How experienced is the trainer?** At least two years of experience is optimal. Choose a personal trainer who has a broad range of experience and can help you cover all the components of a good program: cardiovascular activity, strength training, balance and flexibility training. If you have any special needs, make sure the personal trainer is qualified to work with you. A good trainer will have you complete a health history questionnaire before you begin so that he or she can design a program that will meet your goals and expectations.

4 **Does the trainer know CPR and first aid?** In the event of an emergency, you want someone who keeps up to date in these areas.

5 **Does the trainer's schedule work well with yours?** Choose someone who can work with you on the days and times you are available. Convenience is key.

6 **Make sure the trainer has liability insurance.** Look for a trainer who insures himself/herself against personal injury and property loss.

7 **Ask up-front about the trainer's business policies.** What does he/she charge per hour? As a general rule, the average cost in a metropolitan area is $50 an hour. Yes, the expense is a definite consideration; however, it may help motivate you to exercise, especially on those days when you need a little encouragement. It doesn't have to be an ongoing expense—a half-dozen sessions may be enough to get you going.

8 **Request client references.** Call the trainer's customers to find out his or her strengths and weaknesses.

born to run?

Running is an excellent form of aerobic exercise. It can be done almost anywhere and any time. It takes little skill and only a good pair of shoes and a safe environment. Running burns a high number of calories in a short amount of time. It can be done alone, with a partner or in a group. Though running isn't for everyone, it may be a good option for you if you are a walker and are ready to increase the intensity of your workout.

START SAFE

Talk with your doctor before starting a running program. To run enjoyably and safely requires a moderate to high level of fitness. If you've been inactive for a while, have joint problems or are overweight, it's best to start with a walking program or another moderate activity and then progress to running as your fitness improves. Despite popular belief, running doesn't cause joint problems in most people; but if you are one of the many who suffer from orthopedic or heart problems, or if you are more than 20 percent overweight, you may want to consider choosing another moderate activity.

WHAT YOU NEED TO GET STARTED

The most important equipment is a good pair of shoes. Running in improper or worn-out shoes can cause injuries (however, most running-related injuries are caused by doing too much too soon).

Running Shoes
- Look for lightweight styles.
- They should be well-cushioned in the heel and forefoot.
- Go for plenty of toe room—about a thumb's width between the end of the shoe.
- Try on several pairs before buying—jog in the store or outside to find the pair that fits best.

Clothing
In hot weather:
- Clothing should be lightweight and loose-fitting.
- Light-colored clothing is usually best.
- The new fabrics that "wick away" moisture are excellent.
- Sunglasses, a cap and sunscreen are important.

In colder weather:
- Wear several lightweight layers rather than one heavy layer.
- The inner layer should be a fabric that wicks moisture away from your body.
- Choose an outer layer that blocks the wind and moisture. As your body warms up, you can remove a layer of clothing.
- Don't forget your hat and gloves. Large amounts of body heat are lost through an exposed head.

YOUR DESTINATION

You can run anywhere—in your neighborhood, at the park, on a track or treadmill. Wherever you choose to run, be sure it's convenient, enjoyable and safe. Consider the following when choosing a location:

- Choose a place with little traffic and few obstacles. Always try to run against traffic so that you can see approaching vehicles.

- At night, run on well-lit streets in a familiar neighborhood, and consider taking a partner with you. Always let someone know where you are going and when you will return. Make sure to wear light-colored and reflective clothing.

- A track can be a great place to run. It has a special surface, you're never too far from where you started and you can easily measure your distance. On a regular-sized track, four laps will equal a mile. It's best to run on smooth and flat surfaces to lower your risk of injury.

A SAMPLE PROGRAM

Walk briskly for at least 20 to 30 minutes several days a week before moving on to a running program. When you're ready to begin, consider this plan:

- Begin by running short distances during your walk. Try to work out at least three days each week of the program. If you find a particular week's pattern tiring, repeat it before going on to the next level.

- Progress according to your goals and how you feel. You don't have to complete the program in 12 weeks.

- Individuals who are in good shape may progress at a faster rate by increasing time and intensity simultaneously, while those who are less fit may opt for increasing more gradually.

Running Tip: Increase your pace gradually over a period of several weeks.

	Warm-up (walk slowly)	Walk/run program (walk briskly/run slowly)	Cool-down (walk slowly)	Total time
Week 1	5 minutes	5 minutes/1 minute	5 minutes	20 to 30 minutes
Week 2	5 minutes	4 minutes/1 minute	5 minutes	20 to 30 minutes
Week 3	5 minutes	5 minutes/2 minutes	5 minutes	20 to 30 minutes
Week 4	5 minutes	4 minutes/2 minutes	5 minutes	20 to 30 minutes
Week 5	5 minutes	5 minutes/3 minutes	5 minutes	20 to 30 minutes
Week 6	5 minutes	4 minutes/3 minutes	5 minutes	20 to 30 minutes
Week 7	5 minutes	5 minutes/5 minutes	5 minutes	20 to 30 minutes
Week 8	5 minutes	5 minutes/8 minutes	5 minutes	20 to 30 minutes
Week 9	5 minutes	10 minutes/10 minutes	5 minutes	30 minutes
Week 10	5 minutes	5 minutes/15 minutes	5 minutes	30 minutes
Week 11	5 minutes	20 minutes	5 minutes	30 minutes

Week 12

Once you progress to 20 minutes of running three days per week, consider these options:

- **Stay where you are.** Twenty minutes of running three days per week will give you the aerobic benefits you need for good health.

- **Add another day of walking or jogging.** Start at week 1 and follow the schedule for increasing your time on that day.

- **Increase your pace gradually over a period of several weeks.** One way to increase your pace is to run faster for one to three minutes then slow down for three to five minutes or until your breathing has returned to normal. This is called *interval training.* Start with one interval each workout; then add an interval each week, or when you're ready.

- **Increase your running time by three to five minutes each week** or as you feel ready.

- **Consider cross training with another activity** such as swimming, bicycling or strength training.

STAYING STRONG

Running isn't for everyone. By all means, don't give up on exercise if running doesn't fit the bill for you! If it agrees with you, however, keep in mind these following tips:

- **Run at a pace that feels comfortable.** If running leaves you so short of breath that you can't keep up a conversation, it's too intense.

- **Stay relaxed when you run.** Keep your back straight, shoulders back and head up. Swing your arms freely at about the level of your hips and keep your hands relaxed. Breathe through your nose or mouth naturally. Land on your heel, keep your toes pointed forward, roll your foot forward and push off with the ball of your foot. Maintain a smooth stride and avoid bouncing.

- **Learn some basic stretches** for the lower back, legs, calves and ankles. Do these before and after you run.

- **Drink plenty of water before, during and after your run.** Don't wait until you feel thirsty to drink.

- **Pay attention to your body.** If anything hurts, take time off or slow your pace until it feels better.

- **Pay attention to your surroundings.** Listening to music can be motivating, but make sure it's not so loud that you can't hear an approaching car or another runner.

- **Record your success.** Keep a training diary to monitor your progress.

making
a splash

One great way to add variety and fun to your fitness program is with activities such as water aerobics, water walking and swimming. Water is great for exercise because it:

- provides resistance
- keeps you cool
- supports your body weight

Why water? Check out the benefits:

- It is fun and enjoyable.
- It decreases body fat.
- It improves body awareness, balance and coordination.
- It increases flexibility and muscle strength.
- It improves cardiovascular fitness.
- It is low impact and has a lower risk of injury.
- It improves mood and self-esteem.

WHERE DO I BEGIN?

Here are some ideas to help get you going.

- Simply start at one end of the pool and walk back and forth from end to end.
- To increase the intensity, swing your arms back and forth in the water.
- The deeper the water, the greater the resistance and the more you rely on your balance.
- Buy a flotation vest for deep-water running. Water gloves, water weights and similar equipment can be used to add variety to your workout.
- Rest between laps; keep moving by walking. As you become more fit, you can increase the speed and distance you swim.
- Work up to about 30 minutes of moderate to vigorous movement in the water.
- Use a modified breaststroke or backstroke that allows you to keep your head out of the water. Use a froglike kick for mobility.
- Once coordination and fitness improve, add a freestyle (front crawl) stroke.
- Goggles, earplugs, caps, snorkels and fins may make you feel more comfortable in the water.
- Consider taking lessons. Many community centers, YMCAs and fitness centers offer lessons as well as fitness swimming sessions.

A GOOD ALTERNATIVE

Are you having a hard time finding an activity that suits your specific needs? Consider water aerobics. It's easy on the joints and the back. It's a great choice for pregnant women, people who easily overheat, and those who are obese and want a safe way to be active.

- If you like the water, join a water aerobics class. Many health clubs, YMCAs and community centers offer water-aerobics classes. These classes are designed for all age groups and abilities. Many use the same basic movements as regular aerobics classes. In addition to being a beneficial physical activity, this is a great way to enjoy the friendship that comes from working out with a group.
- When you swim outdoors, remember to wear sunscreen and protective clothing. You're not limited to a traditional bathing suit these days. Many companies make special water wear. Avoid getting too hot or cold.
- Even though you're surrounded by water, don't forget to drink. Keep a water bottle with you so that you can hydrate while you exercise.

ANTIDOTE FOR PAIN

If you battle fibromyalgia and want relief, take heart. Several studies have shown that fibromyalgia patients experience reduced pain, improved functionality and better emotional health as a result of engaging in water exercise.

bicycling your way
to health and fitness

How long has it been since you've pedaled a bicycle? More than likely, you enjoyed bicycling as a kid. Now, as an adult, you can reap the following benefits from this popular sport!

- It is low impact—easy on the bones and joints.
- It strengthens the muscles of the lower body, such as the thighs, hips and buttocks.
- The upper body and arms get a workout when climbing hills or riding a stationary bike with arm levers.
- It can give you a wonderful sense of exhilaration and excitement, especially when you are outdoors.
- It can be done indoors on a stationary bike. Stationary bicycles are relatively inexpensive and can fit in almost any room in the house, providing a way of working out when the weather is bad or your time is limited.

Before purchasing a bike, think about the following questions:

- Do you want to ride indoors or outdoors?
- Do you plan to ride long distances—greater than 20 miles?

- Will you be riding in the neighborhood, on a bike trail (paved or dirt) or on country roads?
- How much money do you want to spend? Bicycles can range from $150 to more than $2,000.

Once you purchase your bike, check it each time before you ride to ensure that it's in good repair.

Outdoor Bicycles

- **Racing bicycles** are lightweight, have narrow tires and dropped handlebars. Most have 10 to 14 gears.
- **Mountain bicycles** are very popular because they can be used on or off road. They have wide tires and upright handlebars, and they provide a softer ride than racing bikes. They have from 18 to 24 gears.
- **Hybrid bicycles** are a cross between a racing and a mountain bike.
- Unless you plan to ride only short distances on flat roads, buy a bicycle with 10 or more gears.

Cycling burns 600 calories in an hour. You can travel three times faster than you can walk for the same amount of energy.

Stationary Bicycles

- Choose a bike with a smooth pedaling motion.
- Make sure that you're comfortable with the pedaling resistance and that it's easily adjusted.
- A comfortable and adjustable (tilt) seat is a must. If bicycle seats are typically uncomfortable for you, look for a recumbent bike that will allow you to sit in a padded chair with your legs extended in front of you.
- Some bikes have arm levers that allow you to work your upper body, too.

The Proper Fit

You are more apt to stick with your exercise program and avoid injuries if you have a bicycle that fits. A specialty shop can help you select a bike that meets your needs.

- The handlebars should be in a position that allows you to relax your shoulders and arms. You should be able to reach the brake levers easily.

- The seat height should allow your knees to be only slightly bent when the pedals are in the lowest position. Position your feet so the balls of your feet are in the center of the pedals. If your seat is too high, your hips will rock back and forth when you pedal. A seat that's too low puts extra stress on your knees.

- The tilt of the saddle should be parallel to the ground. If the seat is tilted downward, you'll have to use your arms to hold your body up. A seat that's tilted too high puts too much pressure on your crotch.

Riding Gear

While not necessary, special cycling clothing can make your ride more pleasant.

- **Shoes** can really make a difference. You can wear a comfortable pair of tennis shoes or choose bicycling shoes. These specialty shoes are lightweight and can improve the efficiency of your pedaling. If you plan to ride longer distances, bicycling shoes are a must. Some pedals and shoes are designed to work together. These take more skill to use because the shoes actually clip directly onto the pedals. Never cycle barefooted.

- **Bicycling shorts** are a good investment no matter what type of riding you plan to do. You can buy tight or loose-fitting shorts with a special pad that provides cushioning, absorbs moisture and prevents chafing.

- **Bicycling shirts** are good for riding outdoors because they're tight fitting and cut down on wind resistance. The newer fabrics pull moisture away from your body. Bike shirts may also have special pockets for a water bottle.

- **Bicycling gloves** improve comfort by providing padding for your hands.

- **Sunglasses or protective eyewear** for the weather conditions is important. Even if the sun is not shining brightly, UV rays can be damaging to unprotected eyes.

> **TURN UP THE HEAT**
>
> If you want to take your fitness to a new level, consider going to an indoor cycling class. Most health clubs offer such classes, and they are popular because you can work at your own pace—and burn *a lot* of calories.

- Carry along one or two **water bottles**. You need to drink water frequently when bicycling. Because of the airflow, you may not realize you're sweating.

Selecting a Helmet

A helmet is your most important piece of equipment. Helmets save lives. Never ride without one!

- The helmet should fit snugly and comfortably.
- It should have adjustable straps that can be buckled below the jaw.
- The helmet must be certified by the American National Standards Institute (ANSI) or the Snell Foundation.

Other safety considerations include avoiding riding in high traffic areas or at night, and keeping your bike in good repair.

A SAMPLE BICYCLING PROGRAM

Try to ride at least three days during each week of the program. If you find a particular week's pattern tires you out, repeat it before going on to the next level. Progress according to your goals and how you feel. You don't have to complete the cycling program in eight weeks. A brisk ride increases your breathing slightly, but not so much that you can't carry on a conversation.

	Warm-up (ride slowly)	Aerobic cycling (ride moderate to vigorous)	Cool-down (ride slowly)	Total time
Week 1	5 minutes	10 minutes	5 minutes	20 minutes
Week 2	5 minutes	12 minutes	5 minutes	22 minutes
Week 3	5 minutes	15 minutes	5 minutes	25 minutes
Week 4	5 minutes	17 minutes	5 minutes	27 minutes
Week 5	5 minutes	20 minutes	5 minutes	30 minutes
Week 6	5 minutes	25 minutes	5 minutes	35 minutes
Week 7	5 minutes	30 minutes	5 minutes	40 minutes

Once you get to 30 minutes of brisk cycling, you may want to consider some new options:

- Add another day. Start at Week One and follow the schedule for the day you're adding.

- Increase your pace gradually over a period of several weeks. One way to increase your pace is to ride faster for one to three minutes; then slow down for three to five minutes or until your breathing has returned to normal. This is called interval training. Start with one interval each workout, then add an interval each week or when you're ready.

- Increase the time you spend riding by three to five minutes each week or as you feel ready.

exercising safely
outdoors!

There are many enjoyable and beneficial activities you can do outside, such as walking, hiking, bicycling, swimming, running, skiing and other recreational sports. However, it's important to consider weather, clothing, equipment and environment. Some activities, such as downhill skiing, in-line skating and bicycling require more precautions for safety. Choose activities that you enjoy, but *play it smart!*

WHAT TO WEAR

Footwear

- A good pair of shoes is the most important piece of equipment for exercising outdoors. The best shoe is the one that fits your foot well, not necessarily the most expensive one.
- Try on several pairs before buying. Does the shoe feel natural when you walk? Keep trying until you find one that feels right! If possible, shop at a store with experienced staff who will help you find the right fit.
- Make sure the shoe supports your arch and has plenty of room for your toes; allow for a thumb's width between your toes and the end of the shoe.

- For walking or jogging, choose a flexible shoe with good cushioning. Don't go hiking in tennis shoes—wear the appropriate boot or shoe.
- For court and field sports, consider a high-top shoe to protect your ankles.
- Wear cotton or nylon athletic socks. It's not necessary to wear a double layer.

Clothing

- Whether exercising in the heat or cold, always wear clothing that can be layered and easily removed or put back on as your body temperature changes.
- Check with a local sports store for the best clothing and protective gear for your activity.
- At night or early in the morning, wear reflective and light-colored clothing, and carry a flashlight.
- Depending on your activity, consider carrying a small backpack or fanny pack to store extra clothing.
- When exercising in the heat, avoid clothing that does not ventilate well, such as rubberized suits or sweat suits. Wearing such clothing is a dangerous practice that can lead to dehydration and heat stroke!

WEATHER

Extreme temperatures affect how your body responds to exercise. High temperatures and humidity, or cold temperatures and wind, place additional stress on your body. Check the weather forecast before heading outdoors. *Always decrease your intensity level and take it slow when it's very hot or cold!*

Tips for Beating the Heat

- It takes 10 to 14 days to adapt to heat. If you're exercising in hot conditions, cut your intensity and duration in half and gradually increase your activity as your body adapts to the heat.

- Drink water before, during and after exercise. Drink at least 5 to 8 ounces of cool water 15 minutes before and then every 15 to 20 minutes during exercise.
- On really hot days, exercise indoors or during the coolest part of the day.
- Wear lightweight, loose-fitting clothes, a hat and sunscreen to protect yourself from the sun. If you wear a hat, make sure it allows for ventilation.

Tips for Surviving the Cold

- Don't rely only on the ther-mometer! Wind chill greatly increases the chill your body experiences. Activities such as roller-blading, ice skating, ski-ing and even running can con-tribute to a heightened wind chill factor.
- Dress warmly and in layers that can be easily removed. Several layers warm better than one heavy jacket. Because phys-ical activity quickly generates body heat, it's important to be able to remove layers as your body heats up.
- Wool and synthetic fabrics are good choices because they wick moisture away from your body. Wear an outer layer that keeps out the wind and moisture.
- Much of your body's heat can be lost through your head and neck, so wear a hat and scarf. Don't forget to protect your hands.
- Watch out for slick surfaces caused by rain and snow.
- It's just as important to drink water in the cold as in the heat—and remember to wear sunscreen.
- When exercising in the cold, stay close to home or other shelter.

HOT WEATHER ALERT

Take precautions when the humidity is above 70 percent and the temperature is above 70 degrees. Such weather conditions can be hard on your heart, warns the American Heart Association. When you sweat, you lose fluid. Your heart has to pump even harder to get a smaller volume of blood to your work-ing muscles, skin and other body parts. Extreme fluid loss can lead to brain and heart damage.

Check your body fluid level the morning after exercising outdoors. If you weigh two pounds less than usual, you may be dehydrated and should drink more water—especially if you plan to engage in more outdoor activity!

A NOTE ABOUT ALTITUDE

Altitude increases the stress of physical activity. It's harder for your body to take in oxygen above 5,000 feet. This means that your heart, lungs and muscles have to work harder. Symptoms of altitude sickness include lightheadedness, dizziness, nausea and unusual shortness of breath. Give yourself a couple of days to get used to the higher elevation, and cut back the intensity of your activities.

staying active
while traveling

W hether traveling for business, a weekend getaway or family vacation, many people find it more difficult to stay physically active while on the road. The good news is that with a little planning, you can enjoy the benefits of activity while traveling. Sure, it may be a little harder to make time for it, but the benefits will be well worth the effort.

BUSINESS TRIPS

When traveling for business, schedules are often tight—meetings run late, flights are delayed and colleagues want to entertain you. The key to a physically active business trip is—you guessed it!—planning. Try the following tips for fitting in activity when you travel on business:

- Get up a little earlier in the morning to fit in some activity; this way you can't miss it! You'll be glad you started your day off right.
- If possible, schedule activity into your day just as you schedule meetings.
- Make sure colleagues know that physical activity is part of your lifestyle.

- When traveling, wear comfortable shoes or carry tennis shoes in your carry-on bag. Walk between meetings or while waiting for your flight—even 10 minutes of exercise will help.
- Fit in activity by taking the stairs instead of the elevator, carrying your own bags and walking wherever you can.

VACATIONS

Traveling for pleasure is a great way to enjoy your health and fitness. Go for a hike in the mountains, walk along a secluded beach, bicycle through the countryside or windsurf over the waves. Don't think so much about following your usual routine; look for new ways to be physically active.

- Local attractions such as parks, zoos, nature trails and other activities can provide opportunities to see the sights and get some activity at the same time!
- Consider active vacations, such as a spa retreat specializing in fitness, a camping trip in a national park or a cycling trip during autumn in New England or even abroad. Stay at hotels with exercise facilities.
- Look for ways to be active with your traveling companions: Rent bicycles, skates or other recreational equipment. Go on walking tours, especially if you're in big cities that offer a guide. It's often easier to stay active if you have the support of others.

WORKING OUT ON THE FLY

A growing number of airports now have fitness clubs either right in the terminal or in hotels attached to a terminal. Las Vegas McCarran Airport even has a stand-alone gym on-site for travelers and airport personnel who want to squeeze in a workout. A number of these gyms offer day passes that cost $15 or less, making it an affordable option for many travelers.

- Find out about the weather conditions before you go so that you can pack the right clothing.
- Take along recreational equipment such as racquets, golf clubs, a jump rope and lightweight dumbbells.

TIPS FOR ACTIVE TRAVELERS

Choose a hotel that will help motivate you to exercise. Questions to ask before you make your reservations:

- Does the hotel provide an exercise room and/or indoor pool?
- Are there safe walking paths nearby?
- Is there a mall nearby where you can walk?
- Are there local fitness facilities you can use?

Be flexible and anticipate changes.

- If the weather is bad, walk in a mall or go to an indoor fitness center.
- For a quick workout, take along elastic exercise bands, hand weights, a jump rope, music or an exercise video for activity in your hotel room.
- If a flight is delayed, take a brisk walk around the airport terminal.

When you travel, avoid overdoing it. Don't push yourself when you're tired. Sometimes your body needs sleep more than exercise. If you have an opportunity to exercise, it may revive you; on the other hand, it can become another stressor. Remember, there's plenty of time for physical activity when you get home.